The Illustrated Bearmas Reader

Ralph's Ordeals

dhtreichler

Illustrated by Grant Boerner

© dhtreichler 2015. All rights reserved

This is a work of fiction. Names, characters, businesses, places, events and incidents are either the products of the author's imagination or used in a fictitious manner. Any resemblance to actual persons, living or dead, or actual events is purely coincidental.

No part of this publication may be reproduced, distributed, or transmitted in any form or by any means, including photocopying, recording, or other electronic or mechanical methods, without the prior written permission of the publisher, except in the case of brief quotations embodied in critical reviews and certain other noncommercial uses permitted by copyright law.

THE ILLUSTRATED BEARMAS READER

Introduction

This work is intended to provide a resource to children and their families, to help them better understand the nature of adversity and the role that family, friends and professionals in every community play to make it easier to cope with their own life ordeals. I also hope it will inspire parents and children to tell their own stories of overcoming challenging circumstances and becoming worthy.

The story of SJ Wilcox and her struggles as recounted in the novel <u>Inspirations</u> is illustrative of similar experiences by millions of children around the globe. We find these individuals in nearly every community and yet most of us are unaware of what they go through and how they must persevere.

The introduction of Ralph the bear and the ordeals the Supreme Bear Council selects for him to prove himself worthy of SJ was an inspiration borne of necessity in the novel. It nevertheless is an opportunity to help others like SJ, as they work through their own ordeals by capturing their imaginations, increasing their understanding of ordeals and the nature of adversity and inspiring and giving them something to look forward to during their own often protracted struggles.

This reader is an illustrated version to help children visualize the stories. I sincerely hope that it serves to comfort and inspire them to endure as Ralph the bear endured to prove himself worthy of SJ.

The Story of Bearmas

Ralph the Bear

Early morning light fills a child's antiseptic hospital room. The television stares blankly at the attractive early twenties mother, Genevieve, who focuses her energy on her seven-year-old daughter, Sarajane, affectionately known by just her initials, SJ.

A very tired-looking but showered and dressed Genevieve sits on the bed next to her daughter. Genevieve's hair remains wet and make-up has not been added yet, but SJ listens, enthralled by the story her mother tells. "And that's how the lion found its tail."

SJ doesn't want her mother to leave yet. "One more, this time about a bear."

"A bear, huh? Let me see…" Genevieve tries to think of a story and while she thinks about it, the forty-ish Dr. Hamilton steps to the door but stops to listen.

"Well … did I ever tell you the story of Bearmas?"

Genevieve doesn't want to get into another discussion about the attic bear that Genevieve's mother will not let SJ play with, so she tries to make this one up as she goes, as she already told SJ all the bear stories she knows at least a million times, or so it seems.

"No, tell me." An eager smile appears on SJ, and Genevieve smiles back, happy to see her daughter excited as her imagination goes to work.

"Well the celebration of the birth of a bear is called Bearmas."

"Why isn't it just a birthday?"

"There's more to the story. Just listen.

"Okay."

"Did you know that when little girls and boys need help or comfort that a bear is born? That bear is intended for that little boy or girl and no one else." As Genevieve begins to tell it, the story begins to flow.

"Like me?" SJ gets more excited envisioning her own bear.

"Yes, just like you." Genevieve kisses her daughter on the top of her head.

"Now that bear has to prove to its parents and the Supreme Bear Council that it is worthy of being the one special bear for that little boy or girl. In order to do this the bear must undergo a whole series of ordeals to prove it."

"What's worthy mean?" SJ tries to take this all in.

"Worthy is when you show that you deserve something. Like I was worthy of promotion at work, but it looks like Andrea didn't agree." Genevieve reflects and SJ gets impatient with her.

"Stick to the bear, Momma. So what's an ordeal?"

"An ordeal is something very difficult to accomplish and very hard to get through because there are all kinds of unpleasant things that happen. Ordeals generally aren't much fun."

"Did you ever have an ordeal, Momma?"

"You don't have ordeals; you go through them because they take such a long time."

"Longer than a movie?"

"Much longer."

"That's a long time. Can you pause it in the middle to go to the bathroom?"

"Let's get back to the story. Okay?"

SJ glances up at her mother but does not respond.

"All right, now let me see. The bear has to undergo a series of ordeals."

"What's a series?"

"More than one."

"How many is that?"

"I'm not sure. Ten, maybe."

"But if ordeals take a long time, when do I get my bear?"

"When your bear has completed them … his ordeals."

"But I want my bear now."

"I know, honey, but you'll have to wait. Can I finish the story now?"

SJ sulks as she listens.

"Some bears do not succeed in all of their ordeals."

"Is that why I don't have a bear?"

"I don't know sweetheart."

"What happens if he doesn't succeed?"

"The bear becomes disgraced and must join the salmon hunters, also known as the redeeming bears.

"What's redeeming?"

"If you don't do something right, you can redeem yourself by doing something to show you are worthy."

"How does my bear redeem?"

Doctor Hamilton enters the room and sits down on the chair to listen. Genevieve gets up, but he motions for her to continue.

"How does my bear redeem, Momma?"

Genevieve hesitates for a moment, with an unexpected audience, she tries to collects her thoughts, distracted by the good-looking doctor, not sure she likes having an audience for the rest of this and knowing she's keeping the doctor from his rounds.

"For a year the redeeming bear must fish for salmon."

"What are salmon?"

"They're big fish found in the most remote rivers of Alaska."

"And why does he have to fish there?"

"To feed all of the northern bear tribes."

"One bear has to feed all the other bears? That doesn't sound fair." SJ observes, trying to understand this story.

"It gets worse. At the end of that year each redeeming bear must then join the baklava bakers."

"What's a baklava?"

"You've had them. They're those little squares I sometimes bring home from the bakery. They're made from nuts and honey and phyllo dough. You like them."

"Can you bring me a baklava?"

"Tomorrow. Now let me finish. So the redeeming bears must gather nuts and honey and make baklava for all of the northern bear tribes."

"Can I be a northern bear?"

"Why would you want to be a northern bear?"

"If I'm not going to get one, maybe I should be one."

Genevieve hugs her daughter. "Sorry. You are what you are, and besides it gets very cold in the far north and you don't like the cold. You told me yourself."

SJ shudders, thinking about the cold.

"After a year making baklava they have redeemed themselves and become eligible to challenge the ordeals for their chosen boy or girl. But this must be their last chance."

"Last chance? What happens to them?" This thought upsets SJ.

"If the redeemed bear successfully makes it through the ordeals, they come and live with their chosen boy or girl. But if the bear fails at even one ordeal, it finds itself cast out of the bear tribes and must wander the wilderness of the most far northern reaches of Alaska."

"That's very sad."

"But think about it. Bears can be small or very big."

"Why is that?"

"Smaller bears successfully complete all their ordeals. But if a much larger bear arrives, then you know that bear did not make it through the first time, but is a redeemed bear."

"Why is it bigger?"

"From eating all the salmon and baklava."

"I don't want a redeemed bear."

"If you think about it, though, redeemed bears have many more stories to tell and are also good salmon fishermen and baklava bakers. And that's why when we celebrate Bearmas, we always eat salmon and baklava in remembrance of the redeeming bears."

SJ's eyes become wide, "Then that bear in the attic must have passed its ordeals the first time because it was a small bear."

"Yes, and was polite and minded its manners, as I remember." Genevieve does not want to stop now, but looks at her watch and starts to get up, until SJ pulls her back down. "So when is Bearmas, Momma?"

"Bearmas can be anytime a boy or girl needs a bear. We don't actually celebrate the day the bear is born, because we don't know if it will pass its ordeals. So Bearmas is a celebration of that bear's birth on the day it passes the last of its ordeals and arrives to live with the chosen boy or girl. Does that make sense?" Genevieve glances at her watch and becomes embarrassed at how long it took to tell the story and how late she will be for work.

Then Dr. Hamilton speaks up. "That was a wonderful story about Bearmas. I'd never heard it before. But Sarajane, you don't have a bear? Why --?"

SJ cuts him off, "SJ. My name is SJ. People only call me Sarajane when I've done something bad."

"Excuse me, SJ. Why don't you have a bear?"

"He must be going through his ordeals." SJ realizes aloud.

"And the ordeals are very dangerous. But I'm sure your bear is very smart, courageous and brave and will succeed." Dr. Hamilton adds.

Genevieve tears up and smiles at the doctor. "I need to get to work..." she feels her hair, "...and I'm a mess. Excuse me please."

Dr. Hamilton shrugs. "You look fine, but I need to look at this young lady for a moment. If you want to finish getting ready, I'll let you know what I find when you're done."

"It will take me more than a moment."

"I'll knock before I have to leave."

"I really appreciate what you're trying to do for us." She holds his gaze for a moment, and then remembers how she looks. *Oh God, I'm a mess and he's the last person I would want to see me this way.* She steps into the bathroom. As she starts to close the door behind herself, she hears SJ ask Dr. Hamilton, "What happens to the boy or girl if their bear is cast out of the tribes?"

"As I understand it, the Supreme Bear Council selects another bear. And that's why sometimes boys and girls wait a long time to get their bear. Now let's take a look at you." The doctor eases into the examination, and Genevieve pulls the door shut.

The Burning Bridge

Ralph on the Burning Bridge

"Well, now let me see if I can remember this." Dr. Hamilton stops for a moment as if to remember. "Doctor Coolidge told me this story just this morning. It seems there was this bear named Ralph. He was selected for a little girl, very much like our SJ here by the Supreme Bear Council. Now he was told by the Grizzly, who is the chairman of the Council, that he has to successfully overcome five Ordeals before he joins his little girl at her Bearmas."

"Five? I thought it was ten ordeals." Genevieve pipes up.

"Ten? I guess it depends on how long you want this to go on?" Dr. Hamilton observes, but then he understands what Genevieve tries to say about SJ and how long she may be in the hospital, and he corrects himself. "No, come to think of it, I think that Doctor Coolidge did say as many as ten ordeals if that's how long it takes for the bear to prove him or herself. Anyway, the Polar Bear who is the Master of Ordeals, pulls a ball from the great Ordeal Mixer that is a lot like one of those lottery machines that has the balls with the numbers on them...."

"She's never seen that." Genevieve lets him know so he won't belabor it.

SJ corrects her mother. "Yes I have. I saw this woman in black pajamas turn on this machine. It had balls that flew through the air. She did something and one of the balls rolled out and it had a number on it."

"Well the Great Ordeal Mixer is a lot like that only when the ball comes out it has an ordeal written on a slip of paper inside the ball. So back to our story. When the Master of Ordeals opens the ball and reads the ordeal to Ralph --"

"What was his first ordeal?" SJ interrupts impatiently.

"The Master of Ordeals read the slip of paper that says only, 'Cross the Bridge of Fire.' And every bear gasped in horror for no bear ever returned from this dreaded ordeal."

SJ gazes off into the distance as if picturing a burning bridge in her mind's eye.

"Well anyway," the doctor continues, "Ralph looks to his father and says, 'I cannot do this. No bear has ever survived the Bridge of Fire.' And Ralph's father looks at his son and says, 'I raised you to do what is right and what is important. You have a little girl that waits for you to prove yourself worthy of her. I believe you are worthy for you are my son. I believe that you will find a way to cross the Bridge of Fire and come back to us. I have taught you many lessons, but the most important lesson is to believe in yourself and to use your imagination to solve problems. I will wait for your safe return.'"

"His father really loves him, doesn't he?" SJ asks with a tear in her eye.

"Yes, he does, but not just his father. Ralph turns to his mother and says, 'Mother I cannot do this. No bear has ever survived the Bridge of Fire.' And Ralph's mother hugs her son and says simply, 'Your father and I believe in you.'"

SJ asks, "Can't they give him a magical weapon?"

Dr. Hamilton replies, "They could, but since his parents are not magicians, they have none to give him."

SJ appears to think about that for a moment, then finally looks to her mother and says, "So how does he get across the Bridge of Fire?"

Dr. Hamilton continues, "So the Master of Ordeals gives Ralph the directions to find the Bridge of Fire and Ralph the bear starts down that road with only the fur on his back and a smile on his face."

SJ interrupts again, "And what color is his fur?"

Dr. Hamilton has to think a moment. "Hmmm. Doctor Coolidge didn't say, but he must have been a brown bear."

"Why?" SJ demands impatiently.

"As a black bear he could sneak up on the Bridge of Fire in the night and cross it in the dark with the Bridge not even knowing he was there. But that's not the way it happened, according to Doctor Coolidge."

"Okay." SJ accepts that explanation.

Dr. Hamilton notices an expression on Genevieve that makes him think she is wondering how she will match this story.

"So Ralph follows the path to the dreaded Bridge of Fire and along the way comes across a farmer putting shingles on his barn. The farmer appears old and tired and asks Ralph for help putting on the shingles. The farmer explains that the fall will soon be upon them, and the rains will ruin the hay if he doesn't have the roof finished. Ralph the bear was taught to do only right and important things. He decides to help the farmer. So he stays for three days carrying up and nailing shingles onto the roof, then on the third night the rains come. But the roof is complete and the hay saved."

SJ becomes impatient. "So he's just putting off going to the bridge like I put off going to bed."

Dr. Hamilton smiles at her admission then contradicts her. "No, he did what was right and what was important. It was right to help the farmer and important that the hay be saved to feed the livestock through the winter. But anyway, the farmer asked Ralph how he could repay his kindness? Ralph tells him that he has to cross the Bridge of Fire as part of his ordeals to become worthy of his little girl. The farmer thinks for a minute and says, 'I know a way. Let me help you.' So the farmer goes to his barn and builds a wheel, a big wheel, as tall as I am, all made of wood."

"What good is a wheel?" SJ wants to know, confused.

"Just listen. He puts shingles around the rim of the wheel and a door into one side. He stands the wheel up on end and tells Ralph, 'If you get inside this wheel at the entrance to the bridge and run inside it so you cross very quickly I think you will make it.' Ralph looks at the wheel and asks why the farmer thinks this will protect him?

"The farmer responds, 'Three reasons, one is by helping me for three days it is now the rainy season and the fire has died down; so it is not as hot. Second, the shingles that will touch the surface of the bridge are made of asbestos and burn very slowly; that will give you more time. And third, if you run very quickly the fire will not have a chance to burn the wood of the wheel'."

Sounding confused, SJ asks, "Isn't that cheating? The farmer's helping him."

Dr. Hamilton smiles again. "No, SJ. It's always better to make friends and have them help solve your problems. No one can always do it all alone."

SJ falls silent, as if thinking, then suddenly says, "Okay."

Dr. Hamilton concludes the ordeal. "So the farmer helps Ralph roll the wheel to the dreaded Bridge of Fire. When they arrive, Ralph becomes frightened and says to the farmer, 'If this is what the fire is like when low, I can't imagine what it's like when it's not the rainy season.'

And the farmer tells the bear, 'In the summer even this wheel would not be fast enough to save you. But now with courage and your greatest effort you can make it.' So Ralph opens the door, climbs in and starts walking the wheel towards the bridge. The farmer sees that he goes too slowly and yells at the bear, 'Faster! Faster!' Ralph hears the farmer's calls and runs inside the circle, and he runs faster and faster. Faster even than he has run in his whole life. And when the wheel hits the dreaded Bridge of Fire, he runs so fast that the flames cannot burn the wood. The temperature inside the wheel rises so high that the bear sweats. The sweat gets in Ralph's eyes, stinging them and he slows as he wipes the sweat away. As he starts running faster again, sweat pours into his eyes once more and again he slows to wipe away the moisture that makes it difficult for him to see where he is going. He picks up the pace again, wiping his eyes as she goes and he fears that he still has a long way to go. But then, he feels the temperature dropping, feels the wheel slowing even with his extra effort, and he realizes that he has started up hill on the other side of the bridge."

"Wow, he did it." SJ rejoices.

Dr. Hamilton puts up his hand to caution her not to celebrate just yet. "But wait. Ralph realizes that he is now on the wrong side of the bridge and that he has to walk for many days to get home. So do you know what that silly little bear did?"

Again appearing confused, SJ shakes her head.

"He starts running backwards, so the wheel will cross back over the bridge, going in the opposite direction. The farmer shouts at him not to try this, it is much too dangerous, but Ralph can only think about completing this ordeal and getting to his little girl sooner. So he runs as hard and fast as he can backwards. But if you've ever run backwards, you know you're slower than when you're going forwards. So, the wheel rolls much slower back across the bridge. Soon, it becomes much hotter and Ralph sweats. The sweat pours into his eyes again so that he can't see where he is going. The fire singes the wood and it burns with clouds of smoke, and still Ralph has crossed only half of the bridge. So do you know what that bear did?"

SJ and Genevieve both shake their heads 'no'.

"He stops the wheel in the middle of the bridge, turns around inside it and then runs again, this time forwards as fast as he can. As he reaches the other side, the farmer tosses a pail of water on the burning wood and quickly opens the door so that Ralph the bear can hop out. So, Ralph is saved with only singed fur around his ankles."

Genevieve smiles at Dr. Hamilton and says, "So the bear passes his first ordeal."

SJ responds, "Yes, twice."

Dr. Hamilton nods, but completes the story.

"The bear was so grateful that he decides not to rush home but stay for another few days and help the farmer build a new chicken coop. 'Thank you, thank you,' says the farmer. 'Now I can raise more chickens.'

"Ralph adds, 'and have more eggs.'

"The farmer thinks for a moment and realizes, 'And more to eat during the cold, cold winter.' The farmer smiles and pats his round, fat tummy.

"Ralph smiles at the happy farmer and decides. 'Yes, definitely, I'll stay.

'Then we must celebrate,' says the farmer, so he and the bear prepare a picnic. They invite the chickens to celebrate, too, and the frogs from the pond, and the bluebirds that nest in the big elm tree. All the rabbits say they'll come, as do the possums and the raccoons and the little brown mice that live snuggled in the hay in the barn. The farmer does not invite the skunk, but he doesn't raise a stink.

The picnic is a big success, and Ralph has more fun than he's ever had before. The blue birds sing while the raccoons and rabbits join in, and the little brown mice hold hands with the frogs and dance around the bond fire. The farmer can't stop laughing, his big, round tummy shaking like Jell-O. Neither can Ralph stop laughing, for we all know how much fun bears have at picnics."

"I think I'm past the barnyard animals." SJ informs the doctor.

"Well…that was how he repaid the kindness the farmer showed him. Then he went home to his mother and father and when they saw him with only slightly singed fur, his mother said, 'We believe in you'. And the bear hugs and kisses his mother and father and gets a good night's sleep."

Genevieve asks her daughter, "So what do you think, kiddo? Good story?"

"Good ordeal, because he passed it."

The Medallion of the Cyclops

Ralph Holds the Medallion

Genevieve tries to pick up the story where it left off. "As I remember, Ralph the bear went home to get some sleep after his first ordeal."

SJ nods agreement.

"So after a good night's sleep he goes back to the Supreme Bear

Council with his parents and watches the Master of Ordeals select another ball from the Great Ordeals Mixer. When the Master of Ordeals opens the ball and reads the Ordeal to Ralph --"

"Is this worse than the bridge of fire?" SJ wants to know.

"The Master of Ordeals reads the slip of paper that says only, 'Bring back the Medallion of the Cyclops.' And every bear gasps in horror for no bear ever returned from this dreaded ordeal."

SJ looks confused. "What's a medallion?"

"It's a piece of jewelry, in this case about four inches across, with a fancy face on it that the Cyclops wears around his neck on a chain."

"Do you have a medallion, Momma?"

"No, kiddo, medallions aren't worn much anymore." Genevieve continues, "Ralph looks to his father and says, 'I cannot do this. No bear ever survived an encounter with the Cyclops. And Ralph's father looks at his son and says, 'I raised you to do what is right and what is important. You have a little girl waiting for you to prove yourself worthy of her. I believe you are worthy for you are my son. I believe that you will find a way to recover the medallion of the Cyclops and come back to us.

"Ralph turns to his mother and says, 'Mother I cannot do this. No bear ever survived an encounter with the Cyclops. And Ralph's mother hugs her son and says simply, 'Your father and I believe in you.'"

SJ looks to her mother and says, "So how did he find the Cyclops?"

Genevieve continues, "So the Master of Ordeals gives Ralph the directions to find the Cyclops and Ralph the bear starts out in search of this beast that wears a medallion around his neck."

"I'll try to make this a little older for you since you didn't like the barnyard animals last time." Genevieve starts out.

"It's not that I didn't like the animals, but I'm seven and I really haven't been into animals for a while now."

Genevieve nods and returns to the ordeal. "Now Ralph has never seen any creature with only one eye, so he was curious at first, but the fear in the voice of the Master of Ordeals gave him pause, and he knows that he too should be afraid. But it is hard to fear something you have never seen. So Ralph takes the road before him and turns just where the Master of Ordeals said that he should."

"Only one eye?" SJ seems to struggle with this idea.

"A big eye, it was. Right in the center of his face." Genevieve holds her hands in front of her own face making the shape of a large round object to help SJ see it.

The little girl pulls back in fright as Genevieve leans toward her with the one eye shaped by her hands. SJ regains her courage and bats at her mother's hands to knock the imaginary eye away.

Genevieve drops the imaginary eye and the devilish grin that appeared with the eye is replaced with a more somber look. Genevieve looks back into her memory as she crafts the next events.

"Ralph looks about him and soon realizes that he entered a deep and dark part of the forest that he has never been in before. But then Ralph has not been many places so any place is probably going to be unfamiliar to him."

"Have you been many places, Granma?" SJ wonders aloud.

"Lots and lots of places, SJ." Her grandmother responds.

"Like where? Have you been deep and dark in the forest?"

Granma colors into a blush, but it passes before she answers. "Many times. In fact, your great grandfather lived on the edge of the forest and when I was growing up I would wander into the deepest and darkest parts of that woods."

"Did you ever find a Cyclops or one-eyed thingy there?"

Granma feigns a search of her memory. She scratches her head and then shakes it. "Not to the best of my feeble memory. Doesn't mean it wasn't there. Just that I didn't see it. Although I remember lots of times when I thought something or someone was watching me and I couldn't see whatever or whoever it was."

SJ shudders at the thought.

Genevieve interrupts the conversation to move the story along. "Now we need to get back to Ralph, he has a long way to go here."

SJ snuggles in closer to her mother. She glances up and seems puzzled by Genevieve's smile.

"Ralph listens to the sound of the hoot owl that seems to be asking who is coming into his woods. Ralph would like to be much smaller so that it is much harder to see him, but that is not to be. Then Ralph thinks it would be good to be much bigger so he would frighten away whatever might be out there. But that is not to be either. Ralph finally abandons his thoughts of changing his size and appearance realizing that he has lost his way and no longer has any idea where he is.

"At that moment a screech owl shrieks and Ralph nearly jumps out of his fur."

SJ thinks about that for only a second, "Don't you mean skin?"

"Well bears have skin that is covered by fur, so I guess he nearly jumped out of both. But that's not the point. Ralph knows this is not going to be easy. He does not have a magic sword. He does not have anything with him to fight a monster, and yet he feels the eyes of something upon him. Something watches him, something that frightened that screech owl."

Genevieve accepts a bottle of water from Dr. Hamilton and takes a sip before going on.

"So all of his senses scan the woods around him, but it is dark and the trees and bushes thick so he cannot see. He listens, but there are so many sounds of animals moving and leaves dropping off trees and the wind blowing that Ralph realizes that something could be right behind him and he might not hear it. And at that moment Ralph thinks he can feel hot breath upon the back of his neck and he spins around and comes face-to-face with an ugly and smelly old troll."

Garth, Troll King of all the Brooks in the Forest

"What's a troll?" SJ looks to her mother for an explanation, but Dr. Hamilton answers for her.

"A troll is a magical character that lives deep in the woods, usually under bridges. The trolls are fierce fighters and protectors of their lands and they generally charge a toll to anyone who wishes to cross their lands or bridges."

"I've never seen a troll. Have you seen a troll, Granma? When you went walking in the deep dark woods?"

"I've seen drawings of trolls, but can't remember ever meeting one."

Genevieve continues. "But anyway, trolls are very nasty characters and you would know that if you ever met one. But Ralph doesn't know this about trolls, so he sneezes because the old troll smells so bad. The troll is perplexed by this behavior as he is used to the forest animals being afraid of him and men showing him respect because of the long knife that he wears in a sheath on his side. But no one has ever sneezed at him before. So the troll just watches Ralph as he tries to regain his composure, but each time as he thinks the sneezing is over, it starts up again and finally the troll moves to his left so he is no longer up wind of Ralph and sure enough, the sneezing stops."

"Why did Ralph stop sneezing?" SJ demands of her mother.

"The wind was behind the troll so it carried the smell that was causing Ralph to sneeze. When he moved to the side, the smell was not so bad."

SJ nods. "That old troll must have smelled really bad."

"Trolls never bathe, so they never get clean. Can you imagine how bad you would smell if you never had a bath?"

SJ sniffs the air in the hospital, but shakes her head, "Worse than my old socks when I play in the mud in the backyard?"

"Oh, much worse than that. Mud just smells dirty. The old troll smelled like year old sweat that has dried on you, mixed in with horse and chicken dung. And worse yet, he never washes his clothes so they trap all that smell and just make it worse."

SJ pinches her nose, "Don't think I'd want to smell that."

"Well, neither did Ralph and that was why he kept right on sneezing until the troll moved away from him. And when Ralph finally stops sneezing, he wrinkles his nose and finally gets a good look at the smelly and ugly old troll. But Ralph is not horrified like most people would be. In fact, he doesn't even think about the fact that the troll has warts all over his face and a long crooked nose and green scaly skin from being so dirty and dry all the time. No, Ralph just looks at the troll and asks. 'Who are you?'

"Now the smelly and ugly old troll is surprised to find a forest creature who does not know who he is, for he is Garth, Troll King of all the brooks in the forest. His legend lives far and wide for he protects his lands and the creatures on them from hunters and fishermen. No one crosses his lands without paying a toll. No one hunts or fishes here without Garth chasing them away with his long and sharp knife. But here is Ralph the bear who doesn't even know who he is.

"Ralph waits and Garth the troll waits, but neither seems willing to make the first move. This too confuses Garth the Troll King. As royalty, he was used to others seeking to satisfy his every whim. Finally the troll grows impatient and asks, 'I could ask the same of you, mister bear.

"Ralph extends his paw to shake as he responds, "I'm Ralph and I must return the medallion that the Cyclops wears around his neck to the Master of Ordeals."

"The smelly old troll's jaw drops at this. 'The Cyclops would never give you his medallion. That is his most prized possession. How do you plan to accomplish this task, Ralph the bear?' And do you know what that bear said to the smelly and ugly old troll?"

SJ shakes her head.

"He said, 'I have no idea.'

"Now Garth the Troll King fought in many battles in the Troll Wars and lived to tell about it, so he made a simple observation. 'It is never a good idea to fight without a battle plan.'

"Now Ralph knows nothing of battles or battle plans, so he, as simply and honestly as he can, asks, "Could you help me with that?" Now, no one ever asked the smelly and ugly old troll to help them before. Everyone always ran away afraid or repulsed by him. They did not look beyond the appearance to see that he really is a wise and kind hearted troll. The forest animals only look at his fearsome scowl and the legend of his many battles. But none ever treated him as a friend or someone who could help.

"The smelly and ugly old troll thought only a moment about the sons he always wanted, but never had as no troll woman would have him for a husband because of his appearance. But then again there are not that many trolls and the forest is very large and he loved his lands so much that he never left them. That made it very hard to meet people and maybe that was the real reason he never had even one son to raise. Anyway, the troll only thought about it for a moment and agreed to help Ralph devise a battle plan.

"The smelly and ugly old troll looked around. 'Where is your army?'

"Ralph did not hesitate in his response, 'I have no army.'"

"The smelly and ugly old troll reacted to this with astonishment, 'then how do you propose to defeat the Cyclops in battle? I have never faced him myself, but I hear tales that he is one of the fiercest fighters in all of the forest, almost as fearsome as myself.'"

"Ralph responds simply, 'I cannot defeat the Cyclops in a battle for I have no weapons and no army.'"

"The troll is even more confused than before, "But that is the only way such things are done in the forest. Armies gather, plans are made to exploit one weakness or another of the enemy and then both sides try to kill as many of the other as possible. Then the winner can claim any prize from the loser he may choose. I cannot see any other way to gain the medallion from the Cyclops.'

"Ralph sits down on the ground to think. 'There must be another way. Is the Cyclops good or evil?' he asks the troll.

"The question confuses the troll. 'He must be evil for he is a Cyclops.'

"Ralph studies the trolls face. 'But you have never talked with the Cyclops so you do not know if he is good or evil?'

"The troll does not even think, but blurts out his response. 'He must be evil for I have never heard anyone say a kind word about him.'

"Ralph considers, 'but would anyone say a kind word about you?'"

"It is clear that the troll had not thought of this. 'I don't know. The animals and fish that I protect, I think they appreciate what I do for them.'

"Ralph gets up and brushes the dirt off his fur. 'Have you ever asked them?'

"The troll's voice drops in realization. 'No. they run off when I appear. I think they too are afraid of me.'

"Ralph takes a step closer to the smelly and ugly old troll, but cannot take his arm as he would like as he is driven back by the overwhelming smell. 'Come with me and together we will take measure of this Cyclops. We will both learn if he is good or evil. If he is good I will reason with him and if he is evil you can engage him in combat and defeat him.'

"Now the troll had heard many stories of the Cyclops in battle. He was not eager to engage him that way as he was said to be easily five times the size of the troll and many times stronger than that. But Ralph shamed him into agreeing to come along. For no King of the Trolls could admit fear. The troll did not know if Ralph realized that or what. But he could not do otherwise than agree to come."

"Did Ralph trick the troll?" SJ asks curiously.

"No. Ralph is not one to trick others, but maybe he understands troll nature."

"Is that like human nature?" Doctor Hamilton asks.

Genevieve smiles like the Cheshire cat as SJ looks back and forth between them. Genevieve then goes on with her story. "Ralph asks, 'Do you know where to find the Cyclops mister troll?'

"Garth, the King of the Trolls cannot admit that he does not know something, so he blusters, 'Of course I know where the Cyclops lives, but he may not be there. After all it is summer vacation time and he may have gone to the beach.'

"Ralph scratches his head. 'I did not know that a Cyclops would go to the beach on vacation. What else do you know about the Cyclops?'"

"The troll is afraid to admit that he did not even know that for sure. It was pure speculation as he really knew nothing about the Cyclops, other than the legends. "The Cyclops is as tall as the trees. It eats a whole cow or a man or a bear at one meal. It prefers meat, but will eat fish if it is prepared with a Veronique sauce and a nice ice cold Sauvignon Blanc.' Now Ralph knows nothing of wines so he is not able to comment on the food pairings, but Ralph did not want to embarrass the troll by asking him a question and he says nothing.

"The troll was quiet for a long moment and began to drool, apparently thinking about that meal. But then he returns to the description. 'Anyway, a Cyclops is a very dangerous creature. He only has one eye, but it bulges from his head and allows him to see things that are to either side of him. Just because he only has one eye, you cannot assume that he will not notice you. The Cyclops also has a keen sense of smell and will actually know you are coming miles away. And because he knows you are coming he sends out the Bat Legions to locate you and try to drive you away before you ever reach his dark and mysterious lair.'"

"What's a Bat Legion?" SJ sounds confused.

"A Bat Legion is a flock of Bats. There are thousands of them in the flock, but they all fly in formation and attack like schooled dive bombers. That's why they call them Bat Legions."

SJ frowns, apparently not completely comprehending the image her mother would have her form, but Genevieve keeps on with the story.

"The troll sees that Ralph is unfazed by the thought of dive bombing bats and a dark and mysterious lair. 'And if you get through the Bat Legions, as you approach the opening to the Cyclops' lair you must climb over a mountain of skulls and bones from the many who have attempted to reach him. The first skulls you find as you approach are of the bears. You see bears are not particularly fearsome to a Cyclops so he generally lets his Pretentious Guard slaughter them with arrows that rain down from the sky in the night so that the bears cannot see them or hear them coming in. The legends say that no bear has ever gotten past the Pretentious Guard.'

"Again, the troll cannot understand why Ralph does not react to this horrible fate that awaits him. 'What do you think about all this, mister bear?'

"As calmly as can be, Ralph responds to the troll, 'I am sure that you will help me find a way to avoid the Bat Legions and the silent but deadly arrows from the Pretentious Guard. After all, is that not your specialty?

"The troll now realizes that he is expected to demonstrate his bravery and decides that nothing is going to deter this bear from his goal. 'Can you lead me there now, mister troll?' Ralph is ready.

"The troll accepts his situation and leads Ralph back to his bridge and into the cave underneath that he fashioned over the years. In the cave are walls of shields, swords, sharp pikes and maces with which to fight. Also Ralph finds jars of nuts and dried fruits, grains and loaves of bread. The troll even has cheeses that he apparently hand made. 'You're a vegetarian!' Ralph exclaimed in sudden understanding.

"The troll looks very embarrassed. 'It's much healthier you know. I wouldn't have lived to be three hundred and eighty-one if I'd been a red meat eater.'

"Ralph nods but has to ask, 'then you're not really blood-thirsty.'

"The troll looks shocked, 'Heavens no. I'm no vampire.'"

"What's a vampire?" SJ interrupts.

"Legend has it that vampires were people who died, but were able to come back to life if they drank the blood of living things." Dr. Hamilton chimes in.

"Why would they do that?" SJ is repulsed.

"It's just a legend, can we keep moving on?" Granma seems to want to finish this story.

SJ nods but with a skeptical look.

Genevieve continues. "So. The troll takes all the shields and swords and pikes that he can carry and leads Ralph out of his cave under the bridge and up onto the road. Up there he looks in both directions before deciding and walks off toward the setting sun with Ralph happily following.

"They walk through the night with the troll watching the skies for the Bat Legions, but none appear. As the sun rises behind them the troll watches the skies for the first hints of the arrows from the Pretentious Guard, but no arrows appear in the sky. So they walk the whole next day with Ralph wishing he could stop for a salmon dinner as his tummy is getting hungry. It has been a long time since he last ate and tummies wait for no bear. Ralph listens for a familiar sound, one that the troll seldom pays attention to. But sure enough, Ralph hears it and wanders into the woods to his left. The troll catches sight of the bear and stops to wait for him. Within a few minutes, Ralph follows the buzz of a bee to a hollow tree. Ralph reaches in and pulls his paw back out covered with honey and a few very upset bees.

"Ralph licks the honey from his paw as he rejoins the troll on the road and of course the bees follow him out of the woods. In a moment the troll swings his shields to ward off the attack of the honey bees. But the bees have little trouble getting through and stinging the troll who races down the road swatting at bees and occasionally dropping another sharp pike. Ralph just sits in the road, licks the honey as the bees buzz angrily about his head, but his thick fur protects him from their stings.

"When he finishes, Ralph rises, brushes off the road dust and follows the road in the direction the troll and the stinging bees went.

"After sunset Ralph finds a pile of swords, shields, sharp pikes and maces next to a pond. He does not see the troll, but after a minute the troll's head rises up in the pond.

The troll listens and looks around. 'Are they gone?'

"Ralph surveys the area and responds, 'I think so.'

"Cautiously the troll steps out of the pond and picks up his collection of weapons. 'I hope you enjoyed your snack. I'm stung from head to toe.'

"Ralph looks at the mud covered troll. 'You went to the right place. The mud is the best thing you can do for a bee sting. It pulls out the poison and you'll be right as rain in the morning.'

"The troll learns something quite by accident but is glad that he will soon feel better than he does at the moment. Since the troll rested in the pond waiting for Ralph to catch up, he is ready to keep walking through the night. Ralph on the other hand is tired from his long walk, but decides that he needs to find the Cyclops before the troll gives up the quest and returns home.

"About midnight the Troll stops walking and motions for Ralph to be quiet. He hands Ralph a shield and takes one for himself. 'Quickly … get under this.' The two drop to the ground, hold the shields above them. The Bat Legions fall from the sky in a thunderous hail storm, bouncing off the shields, picking themselves back up and winging away as if dazed from the impact on those hard shields.

"The storm continues for what seems hours and then just as suddenly as it began the waves of bats end and all is silent. After a few minutes the troll is the first to peek out from under his shield. He scans the sky, listening and watching, but finally trusts that the storm is over and crawls out looking at the sea of stunned bats covering the ground for as far as the eye can see. 'It's over mister bear.'

"Ralph also crawls out from under the shield and likewise surveys his surroundings. The troll picks up his weapons, including the shield that protected Ralph. 'We need to get away from here before they recover.' The troll advises and leads the way stepping gingerly around the bats.

"Just before dawn they arrive at the mountain of bones. Just as the troll foretold, the skulls are those of bears and beyond them all kinds of animals. They begin to climb over the mountain of bones when the first arrows begin to rain down behind them. They quickly scramble through the bones, watching the arrows fall further and further behind.

"Soon they come to the mouth of a huge cavern. The opening must be at least twenty-five feet tall and bones are strewn into it. The troll looks at Ralph who looks back and shrugs. Ralph leads the way into the cavern with the troll racing past so that the bear is not ahead of him.

"The cavern is dark, but candles light the way at intervals. Side passages go off into darkness and they follow the candle-lit path. The bones become further and further apart and soon no bones can be found along the path. Then they hear sounds ahead, unlike any sounds either has heard before. It sounds like an irregular motor turning first in one direction and then in the other.

"Suddenly they enter a huge chamber with a sixty inch plasma screen television, a massive four poster bed with canopy, a tall wine cellar next to a tapped beer keg and a barbeque pit. In the bed is a massive figure with its back to the room. The troll quietly puts down all of his weapons save a single sword. Together they silently creep up to the bed and find a chain around the neck of the sleeping giant.

"Since Ralph does not have fingers, he motions to the troll to undo the chain clasp, which he does. The troll reaches forward and finds the medallion, pulls the chain from under the Cyclops' neck and steps back handing the prized possession to Ralph. They tip toe back to the pile of weapons and the troll has only just picked up his shield when the Cyclops stirs, rolls over revealing his singular eye, which suddenly is wide open staring at them both.

"The Cyclops roars. 'What are you doing in my lair?'

"Ralph, always the brave one, holds up the medallion and responds. 'I have come for the medallion. The Master of Ordeals charged me with returning with it so that I may prove I am worthy of a boy or girl. With my friend the troll, we have overcome all of your obstacles and succeeded in removing it from you while you slept. We are leaving now and expect you to give us safe passage.'

"The Cyclops sits up in his bed, rubs the sleep from his face and looks closer at Ralph, who holds the medallion aloft so the Cyclops can see it better. The Cyclops rises to his full and fearsome height, lets out an earth shaking bellow and then looks at the troll. 'You are the one they call Garth, are you not?'

"The troll has soiled himself, although with his hygiene problems, no one notices. 'Yes. I am Garth, King of the Trolls. Protector of the brooks and the woods and the lakes. Every living thing in the forest fears me.'

"The Cyclops nods. 'I have heard the legends from the troll wars. You are a brave troll.'

"Neither the troll nor Ralph can tell what the Cyclops thinks at that moment, but the troll sheaths his sword and picks up a pike. Ralph steps back and holds the medallion close.

"The Cyclops begins to smile. 'You prepare for battle even though you cannot win. The bear refers to you as a friend, but I have never heard anyone refer to a troll as a friend. Indeed there must be magic amongst you that you survived the Bat Legions and the Pretentious Guard and removed my most precious possession without even waking me.'

"The Cyclops holds up his hand, the medallion leaps from Ralph and flies across the room to the tall beast. He kisses the medallion and tosses it back to Ralph who catches it with both paws. 'As you wish, you may leave my lair, never to return. I give you the medallion to present to the Master of Ordeals as you have demonstrated that you are indeed worthy of a little boy or girl. But you must always remember that ordeals are shared experiences and that one can only survive them when you work together, building on each other's strengths.'

"The troll quickly gathers his weapons and runs for the door, but Ralph remains behind for a moment longer. 'You are indeed a wise and gracious Cyclops and while you only have one eye with which to gaze upon the world, you see the very heart and nature of things.'

"The Cyclops responded to Ralph, 'That is the curse of being a Cyclops. I must look longer and harder to see what you can with your two eyes. I must solve puzzles with less information than you. I must see what you do not by listening and hearing what is not said. You would be wise to learn to do the same."

"The Cyclops sits down on his bed as Ralph, carrying the medallion, follows the troll back to the mouth of the cavern. "I don't know how you did that, but we are fortunate to escape with our lives.' The troll exclaims amazed.

"Ralph gives his friend a knowing smile and together they make their way back through the woods to troll's bridge. There they part company with Ralph giving the troll the chain that held the medallion around the Cyclops' neck. The troll gives Ralph a short sword in a sheath with a belt that he wears around his waist.

"Before returning to the road home, Ralph turns to the troll. 'Be safe my friend, for truly you are my friend. Without your help I would not have demonstrated my worthiness. You are the reason that I will someday make a little boy or girl happy again. Thank you.' Ralph gives his friend a bear hug. The troll has never experienced such a sign of affection and is speechless.

"Ralph waves from the trail and notices a tear streak the troll's face."

Ending the Fairy Wars

Tatiana, Commander of the Fairyland Raiders

SJ waits impatiently for Dr. Hamilton to arrive. It's time for another ordeal. Dr. Hamilton promised that he would stop by this evening and it is now much later than anyone expected and she knows that her mother will want her to go to sleep soon. The nurses poke their heads in periodically looking to see if the doctor has arrived. The ordeals have become the talk of the hospital and it is clear to SJ that the nurses want to hear the stories that the doctor tells her.

Genevieve seems distracted too, as if she were hoping to see the doctor. She keeps fussing with her hair and wrapping a lock behind her ear. When her mother does that SJ knows she is nervous about something. That is one of those things that only appear under certain circumstances and SJ realizes that her mother probably doesn't know that she does it.

Then she hears his voice in the hall and a smile appears on her mother's face. SJ wonders why this doctor seems to make her mother feel better when he hasn't done a very good job of making her feel better. *Another mystery to solve before I go back to school in the fall, even if it will be a new school with different kids.* New friends to make, she can hear her Granma say.

Dr. Hamilton comes in and several of the nurses follow him in and line up along the wall to listen. Dr. Hamilton turns to look at them. "What's this?"

The older charge nurse looks at the others and simply responds, "We heard this was the best entertainment in the hospital. Just wanted to get in on a good thing."

Dr. Hamilton nods and goes to SJ to take a look. "So you ready for another ordeal?"

SJ nods and looks at Genevieve who smiles self-consciously and avoids eye contact with the doctor. He seems to notice this but sits down at the foot of SJ's bed, looks around as if trying to remember something and then begins with a smile.

"So, Ralph waited a week before he was able to return to the Supreme Bear Council with his parents. He watches the Master of Ordeals select another ball from the Great Ordeals Mixer.

"When the Master of Ordeals opens the ball and reads the Ordeal to Ralph –"

"I can't imagine what would be worse than the Cyclops." SJ remarks to her mother.

"The Master of Ordeals reads the slip of paper that says only, 'End the Fairy Wars.' And, every bear gasps in horror, for no bear ever ended a war, let alone one amongst the fairies.

SJ gazes off into the distance with a perplexed look as if trying to picture fairies at war in her mind's eye.

"Well anyway," Dr. Hamilton continues, "Ralph looks to his father and says, 'I cannot do this. No bear ever stopped a war by himself. And Ralph's father looks at his son and says, 'I raised you to do what is right and what is important. You have a little girl that waits for you to prove yourself worthy of her. I believe that you will find a way to end this needless war and come back to us.

"Ralph turns to his mother and says, 'Mother I cannot do this. No bear ever ended a war. And Ralph's mother hugs her son and says simply, 'Your father and I believe in you.'"

SJ looks to her mother and says, "Why are the fairies fighting?"

Dr. Hamilton continues, "So the Master of Ordeals gives Ralph the directions to find the fairies."

"As Ralph leaves the Hall of the Supreme Bear Council he remembers the many stories that his mother told him as a young bear. The stories often recounted the exploits of wizards and goblins, witches and werewolves, but she seldom told him of the fairies. He realizes that he really doesn't know much more about fairies than that Tatania was a good fairy and that she loved Peter Pan. He knows this will not help him in his current quest. He certainly did not know that fairies raised armies. He thought they were friendly types and always willing to help a lost soul in the woods or perform some magical feat. The thought of a fairy war was just simply beyond his comprehension. How do fairies fight? Do they cast spells? Do they sprinkle fairy dust and just watch their opponents float off into space? As Ralph thinks more about it, he isn't even sure they have wings and can fly. Although Tatania did, and since that is his only reference point, he thinks that probably is the case."

SJ gains a cross expression. "Of course fairies can fly. Doesn't Ralph know anything?"

Dr. Hamilton gages SJ's anger and decides he needs to adjust his story. "Of course Ralph knows many things. Do you know how to catch a salmon in a stream with your 'bear' hands?

SJ's anger lessens and she defensively responds, "Not with my 'bear' hands cause even bears don't have hands."

"That's right, they have paws, don't they?"

SJ nods as if confirming she is smart after all.

"So Ralph knows many things, he just doesn't know much about fairies and at this point he wishes that his mother had told him more stories about them so he would have a better idea of what to expect on this ordeal. But Ralph remembers what his father always said in such instances, 'It is what it is.' Ralph thinks about that for a moment and tries to decide if there is anything that he can do to learn more about fairies before he finds himself in the middle of their war. But think as much as he can, he does not come up with an idea of how to do that."

"He should ask me. I know all about fairies." SJ pronounces proudly.

"I didn't know that." Dr. Hamilton observes. "Tell me about their armies and how they fight."

SJ looks less sure, glances as her mother who shrugs and then contritely responds to the young doctor. "My fairies don't fight. They're good fairies."

"Do you think that all the people in the Army are bad people because they fight?"

SJ looks to her mother to save her from this line of questioning.

Genevieve sees her daughter's plight and responds, "Of course not. People go into the Army to protect their country. They are good people doing their patriotic duty."

Dr. Hamilton nods. "It's the same for the fairies. They are good, but when they are threatened, they band together to protect each other. They don't want to fight. They don't want to hurt anyone or anything. But they find themselves in a situation where if they don't protect themselves, their families and friends will either be hurt or maybe die."

Dr. Hamilton sees that SJ does not understand, so he takes a different tact. "Let's say you're at a playground, climbing on a jungle gym and a man comes along and says to you, 'This is my jungle gym. From now on you and your friends cannot play here.' What would you do?"

SJ does not hesitate for even a moment, "I'd ask Mommy to tell him he can't do that."

"Okay. Suppose your mother tells the man he can't do that and the man responds, 'This is my park and you can't bring your family here to play anymore. What would your mother do?"

Again SJ doesn't know how to respond and Genevieve does for her. "I'd ask for proof that he owns the park."

"And if he says he doesn't need to give you any?"

Genevieve answers automatically. "I'd find a policeman."

"And the man would bring his gang and threaten the policeman. The point of the story is that if someone takes away something that you think is yours, you have to get others involved to resolve it and sometimes it takes everyone to defend it. The people who fight wars are good people. Most simply want to defend their families and friends. And that's the way it is with the fairies. They got into a war because one group of fairies wanted something that another group of fairies had."

"What did the fairies want?" SJ demands to know.

"Fairy dust. You see one year there was a shortage of fairy dust and since all the fairies need it to fly, those who did not have enough decided to take it from another group of fairies. In fact, the one group of fairies used all the fairy dust they had to fight the war, so all the fairy dust they had was what they took from the other group. Now the group of fairies that had their fairy dust stolen had to form an alliance with another group of fairies to obtain more fairy dust so they could defend themselves from the first group of fairies.

"All the fairies are good…" the doctor begin.

"No they aren't. That first group stole fairy dust from the others. They're bad fairies." SJ doesn't like this story and it shows.

"No. The fairies are all good. It's just that because of the shortage of fairy dust, some did a bad thing. Up to that point they have always been good and kind fairies, helping lost souls in the woods and performing magic to make the lives of others better."

"But it's wrong for them to steal the fairy dust."

"Yes. It is wrong and the second group of fairies should have found a better way to get the fairy dust they needed. But fairies, just like people, often do not do what is right. If people always did what is right there would be no wars. There would be no crime. Everyone would be happy and have all they need. But unfortunately that is not the reality of the world. And the world of the fairies is no exception.

Genevieve gives SJ a quick hug and the young girl responds still angrily, "It's still not right. Those fairies should be punished."

"How would you punish a fairy that stole another's fairy dust?" Dr. Hamilton asks the frowning young girl…

"I'd make it return the fairy dust and send it to bed without any supper and no TV for at least a week." SJ responds in a maternal tone.

"Well, the fairies are not as wise as you about punishment. And because they are not, they let this get out of control and soon it is fairy nation against fairy nation. And even in a shortage of fairy dust, they are now using most of what they have to fight the war and not to help lost souls in the woods and perform magical feats to help all the creatures of the forest."

"Does Tatania still love Peter Pan?" The unexpected question only causes Dr. Hamilton to miss a single beat. "Yes, she does, but even Tatania finds herself having to choose sides to protect her fairy dust and be able to watch over Peter Pan and perform magic from time to time to help him. Now Tatania is a leader of the Fairyland Army. It's a small army as armies go because there aren't very many fairies in Fairyland. But all the same, now that there is a war that has to be fought, Tatania finds that she no longer has time for Peter Pan and his unending battles with Captain Hook. She has to organize the troops, train them in tactics..."

"What's a tactic?" SJ again loses the thread.

"A tactic is a plan on how to respond to something the other side does and how to implement a strategy." Dr. Hamilton sees the question on SJ's face and responds before she asks. "And a strategy is an approach that you take to achieve your goals or dreams." Dr. Hamilton sees that SJ continues to struggle with all this, but she finally accepts what she doesn't know and her expression changes from confusion to anticipation.

"So what happened to Ralph?" SJ reminds him.

"Ralph? Well as I remember, we left our hero, Ralph the bear, wandering into the forest one more time, wondering why he really doesn't know much about fairies.

"And I said I know all about them."

"That's right. So, Ralph listens to the creepy forest wind blowing through the trees, rustling the leaves and masking the movements of the many forest creatures. Now Ralph knows that something, and more likely, many creatures are watching him in his quest to find the fairy wars. He would like to stop and ask the unseen creatures where he should go look to find the fairies, but since the creatures continue to remain out of sight, he does not. Instead, he continues walking, humming softly and watching the forest get denser and darker."

"But Ralph's been in the forest his whole life. He should be used to it by now."

"Are you used to the first few minutes after the lights go out in your bedroom at night?" Dr. Hamilton responds.

"It's scary until I go to sleep." SJ admits.

"It's the same for Ralph. No matter how many times he enters the forest, it's always scary until he gets used to it, and even then, he carefully listens and watches and is always on his guard for the unexpected."

SJ shudders in response to the doctor's description. He notes this and moves on.

"So, Ralph wanders deep into the forest. Since he does not know where he will find the fairies he decides it doesn't make any difference where he wanders to. He follows the path before him and really doesn't mark the path or do anything that will help him find his way out. He doesn't have a plan for how he will return as he realizes that he will probably do so by a very different trail than the one he takes today."

"Can I have my juice?" SJ points and Genevieve retrieves it for her. The doctor waits for her to finish before he continues.

"I take it you're anxious for Ralph to find the fairies." Dr. Hamilton observes.

SJ nods her agreement.

"So, Ralph comes to a beautiful pool of water deep in the heart of the dark and creepy forest. A brook runs into it and the sound of gently running water fills the air. Ralph senses that this is a magical spot and hopes that a fairy or two might appear. He leans over the still waters to take a drink and when he raises his head from the water he sees a reflection of someone behind him. Quick as a flash, Ralph rises up and spins around to find that he is face-to-face with his friend ... Garth the King of the Trolls. 'Garth! What are you doing here in the deepest and darkest part of the forest?'

"Garth responds with surprise and an anxiousness that Ralph does not remember. 'Ralph. Which side are you on?'

"Ralph does not understand the question, glances around and guesses. 'Your Southside?'

"The troll rapidly scans the area as he answers. 'Wrong question. Whose side are you on?'

"Ralph does not hesitate. 'Why yours of course.'

"Garth hears something and brings his shield higher. 'Then you're with Tatania and the Fairyland Raiders. You chose the right side. I'm pleased to see you wearing the sword I gave you. It will serve you well in the coming battle.'

"Ralph checks the sword on his belt, realizes that he has never removed it from the sheath, removes it part-way to be sure it is all there, then looks up at his friend. 'What's going on here?'

"The troll hears something and signals for Ralph to be quiet. In a moment a beautiful tiny fairy floats in on rapidly beating wings. She stops just a few inches from Garth's face. 'Thunderclap divided his troops and is trying to attack on both flanks simultaneously. It leaves a weak middle and I know we can break through, but we have to leave skirmish troops back to alert us where and when they are coming from behind.'

"Garth shakes his head. 'Better to attack the flanking forces than to go head on with those who are dug in and have established defenses, Tatania. Create a small diversionary attack on one end of their line, but have your main forces seize the initiative and destroy those troops attempting to flank. They will have few defenses up and will not be expecting you.'

"Ralph listens to this discussion and blurts out, 'You make this sound like a game, but it's not. Fairies will die.'

"Both the words and the emotion of hatred underlying Tatania's response surprises Ralph. 'Good. More fairy dust for us.'

"Ralph shakes his head. 'You can't mean that. You can always find more fairy dust, but you can never replace a fallen fairy.'

"Garth provides a measured response to Ralph. 'You don't understand, my friend. Without fairy dust the fairies have to walk everywhere. They can't fly up into the flowers where they gather the pollen and nectars that are their food. They can't perform the magic that comforts the creatures of the forest. Without fairy dust it would be the end of civilization as we know it.' Tatania nods in agreement.

"Ralph sits down to think. In only a moment the answer comes to him. 'But there is plenty of fairy dust. It's just that you have not learned to conserve and share it until the shortage is over.'

"Tatania responds quickly. "The shortage will never be over. There is only just so much fairy dust and when it's gone, it's gone.'

"Still seated, Ralph thinks again for a moment and then responds. 'But there must be alternatives to fairy dust. Maybe you can make alternative fairy dust from reprocessed plant nectar or reconstituted Queen Anne's lace.'

"Tatania's fairy dust is running low so she lands on Garth's shoulder before she loses too much altitude. She looks at Garth as she asks, 'Is he your friend? He certainly has a lot to learn,' Tatania looks directly at Ralph. 'Fairy dust alternatives are just another fairy tale. They cost too much and take too long to make. They also haven't figured out how to make enough to have an impact. Any fairy who expects to continue doing their job and intends to rely upon alternatives is smoking something.'

"Ralph thinks some more. 'Have you done your job since the war began?'

"Tatania's eyes narrow. 'What do you mean?'

"Ralph leans his head to the left to strike a thoughtful pose. 'I assume you are using all of your fairy dust to fight the war. With the shortage you must be rationing it. That would not leave any to do normal fairy things.'

Tatania sounds angry. 'What are you trying to say, bear?'

"Ralph rises and dusts himself off. 'That the war is consuming all your resources and all that you will need for the future. In a war, no one wins and you are mortgaging the future of your children. How long before you save up enough fairy dust to return to your former life? Never. You have changed your society. Now there will be fairies who have fairy dust and fairies that do not. Isn't it better for all fairies to learn to do with less and still enjoy normalcy within limits?'

"Tatania shakes her head. 'No. The Fairyland Raiders will not have to live with limits. It takes away our freedom. We should be able to live the idyllic lives we have always lived.'

"Ralph continues to brush off the road dirt, does not look at Tatania. 'But the world has fundamentally changed, Tatania. We no longer live in an age of limitless existence. We must find ways to live together in peace and harmony and share the resources. Only when everyone can enjoy the same benefits of living in our world will we all find the idyllic existence you remember, but no longer enjoy, because you are too busy trying to regain that which you have already lost.'

"Tatania looks at Garth. 'Is he one of those new age guys? I thought they were all just fairies and that they were all killed at the battle of Fairyland Sea.'

"Garth looks sadly at Ralph. 'It must be a disease, Tatania. Looks like it jumped species. Guess we will have to quarantine him to make sure it doesn't infect the troops.'

"Tatania shakes her head. "I say we just kill him. That way it can't spread."

SJ cries out, "No. You can't kill Ralph. He's a good bear."

Dr. Hamilton smiles at SJ before he continues. "Yes he is a good bear, but let's see what happens, shall we?"

SJ nods, but her eyes are red and moist. She hugs Genevieve fearful for the outcome.

"Ralph does not answer Tatania, but has a heavy heart that reason and logic seems to have no effect on the fairy warlord. Even Garth does not seem willing to come to the aid of his friend. But just then, Tatania opens the sack of fairy dust that she carries attached to her sash and she reaches inside. 'Oh, no. I'm out.' She exclaims. 'I'll have to wait and hope the others have enough for me.' Garth looks surprised, but quickly hides it. Ralph stands waiting for other fairies to arrive. But they wait a long time and nothing happens. The sun goes down and no fairies arrive to help Tatania.

"Ralph gets tired of waiting so he suggests to the others, 'Why don't I gather some wood and we can have a nice fire and some dinner.'

"Tatania observes, 'Fine for you, but I don't eat what you do.'

"Ralph winks at Garth, 'Not a problem, Tatania. If Garth will carry you over to those beautiful flowers you can feast on the abundance of nectar. I'll build a fire to keep us warm and gather nuts and honey for Garth and myself. If we work together we can all rest comfortably for the night and wait for your troops to come and kill me tomorrow.' And that is what they did. Ralph built a small fire with kindling and gathered nuts and berries and brought them back to the fire to share with Garth. Then he went further into the woods and found a honey tree. He dipped his paw in and carried his honey covered paw back to the fire as well. There, he and Garth licked the rich dark honey all off and when they finished, Ralph washed his paw in the mirror-like pond.

"Tatania lay down, not too close to the fire, but close enough to stay warm as wearing a simple leotard does not keep her warm through the night. Garth and Ralph eat the berries and nuts and talk about their ordeal with the Cyclops. Tatania listens to their war story and when they are through she remarks, 'That's a nice story. No one dies and Ralph proves he is worthy.'

"Garth looks at Ralph as he continues the thought. 'And we worked together to do it. Neither of us could have defeated the Cyclops alone, we built upon our strengths to achieve what we all wanted.'

"Ralph let that thought be the last of the night before he curls up in front of the fire, and after a long period of seeming to be, while he thought of ways to end the conflict, he finally went to sleep."

"I don't think I could sleep if someone was going to kill me in the morning." SJ reaffirms that she is following the story.

"I might have a little trouble with that myself." Genevieve chimed in as she studies the doctor, clearly curious about how this is going to end.

"Not me. Nothing keeps me from a good night's sleep. That's one good thing about getting older. None of this means nothing. We all know you can't have an unhappy ending so let's just cut to the chase." Granma acts anxious to get on to something else.

"Ralph woke up several times during the night only to find that Tatania is usually awake, watching for her troops to arrive and Garth is fast asleep, in a dreamless sleep much as trolls, who have seen much too much in their lives, experience. It is almost as if they do not allow themselves to dream about what they have seen or done for fear that they will never be able to dream about anything else should they do so."

"I have the same dream a lot." SJ notes to no one in particular.

Surprised, Genevieve asks, "And what is that dear?"

"I dream of looking at something magical out my window, and when I reach for it, I fall. Only I never stop falling."

Dr. Hamilton glances up quizzically at Genevieve, who returns the look as if hoping for an interpretation, but the doctor is hoping for some insight from her that he can see is not forthcoming.

"Are you frightened?" The doctor asks.

"No. It's a very slow fall, like I'm floating and not really falling at all."

"Does the fall ever end?" The doctor follows up.

"No. I wake up before it does."

Dr. Hamilton nods in understanding, looks at an anxious Genevieve for a moment and then resumes the story. "Ralph listens each time he awakens, hoping to hear the sound of a million fairy wings descending to carry him to his fate and end his period of waiting. But no such sound greets him. In fact, the sounds of the forest creatures seem to have blended into an uncomfortable silence, as if something were lurking in the woods and the creatures are all waiting for it to take its prey and get on with life ... and death.

"When the morning light began to illuminate the horizon Ralph stretches and stifles a yawn. He is not rested, by any means. It was a restless sleep and he knows that today will not only determine his fate, but also the outcome of the fairy wars, of that he is sure. Even though nothing suggested that will be the case, there is no question in Ralph's mind.

"Tatania sits with her back to a tree, but her head rests upon her chest with her eyes closed. Garth's snoring is what probably woke Ralph, but he cannot remember and he is much more interested in a rustling in the forest that he does not recognize. It is both distant and close, hushed, but unmistakable. Ralph watches for some sign of the source of this curious sound and whether Tatania and Garth would awaken before it reached their location.

"And then they are there. All around them at once, marching, not quite like a military regiment, but in a distinctly organized fashion. Fairies. Hundreds, no thousands of fairies fill the clearing from all directions. Most collapse to rest and those behind stumble on them and fall head over heels. It is a most remarkable sight for a bear not used to the ways of the magical woods, having grown up in the humdrum ordinary woods near the towns of the people.

"And still Tatania and Garth sleep on. Ralph asks the fairy closest to him, who is now prostrate with exhaustion. 'What's happened?'

"The fairy looks up at Ralph as if it were an ordinary occurrence to talk with a bear, and answers quite clearly for a very tired fairy. 'No more dust.'

"And of course this only piqued the interest of this big brown bear. 'What ever do you mean?'

"The response is quick in coming. 'Just what I said brother bear. We are completely out of fairy dust. We cannot defend ourselves and must be ready to surrender to the heathen fairies.'

"Ralph has not head this term to describe fairies and wants to satisfy his curiosity. 'What do you mean, heathen?'

"The fairy closest has now recovered enough to have a conversation, which, if you know fairies, is something they take great pride in having. 'Those we have been fighting. They are not true believers. They actually think that fairy dust is not divinely provided and we can make our own.'

"Ralph did not know that fairies divide into different groups. This is the first time he had ever heard about true believers. He thinks about this for a moment and without thinking says, 'Oh. You're talking about the New Agers.'

"Almost instantaneously, as if all the fairies are one, a collective gasp fills the woods. It is enough to wake the sleeping Tatania and even cause Garth to turn over in his sleep. Tatania focuses and after a moment to gather her wits rises and calls out to her troops. 'Friends, Fairylanders and countrymen, lend me your dust, for I have no more with which to carry on the fight.'

"With this call to arms, none of the fairies will look at Tatania. She instantly senses the mood of her troops. 'What's wrong? Why do you turn away?'

The fairy closest to Ralph seems to be a lieutenant of Tatania and stands to address her commander. 'Your brilliance. We do not have fairy dust to share.'

"Tatania waves this away. 'Surely for your commander and comrade-in-arms … you could find…' But Tatania sees that no one will return her gaze. 'What is it?'

"The lieutenant finishes her original thought. 'We do not have any fairy dust amongst us at all. We have exhausted our supplies fighting the war.'

"Garth comes to his senses as the lieutenant finishes her report. 'Then we must build defenses to protect ourselves.' The troll rises to his feet and unsheathes his sword holding it high over his head.

"But the lieutenant shakes her head and looks directly at her commander. 'I don't think that will be necessary either, your brilliance.'

"Tatania reads this situation and calls for a final validation of what she thinks is happening. 'So the heathens are out of fairy dust as well?'

"The lieutenant finally summons the courage to look Tatania in the eye. 'It will take us and them a decade to rebuild supplies to the pre-war levels. And that is only if we manage them carefully.'

"Tatania reads between the lines. 'You're talking rationing?'

"The lieutenant, completes the ugly report. 'Yes, unless we adopt the artificial production methods of the heathens. If we were to do that we could match them ounce for ounce. If we do not they will quickly surpass our production and will be able to re-engage us in war in about five years.'

"Ralph notes, 'No war for at least five years and probably not even then if you match their production.'

"Garth exclaims, 'How awful, no war for five years.'

"And Ralph responds, 'How wonderful. Guarantee of no wars for five years and possibly longer. Sounds like a no-brainer to me.'

"Garth approaches Ralph. 'What are you supposed to bring back this time?'

"Ralph responds, 'A signed copy of the declaration ending the war. I'll help them draft it right now.' Garth nods and goes to prepare the parchment upon which the final declaration will be signed by all parties. And knowing of Ralph's need for a copy he prepares the copy as well.

"The next day the parchment agreement to end the war is signed into law by the leaders of both groups, the New Agers and the Traditionalists. Ralph is presented a beautiful embroidered copy by the Deputy Commander of the Fairyland Rangers. Ralph tucks this document into the belt with the sharp sword given him by Garth, even though he has never used it. He says goodbye to the fairies, and to

Tatania. The goodbye to Garth takes a little longer. Ralph presents him with a silver chalice full of nuts and berries. Garth presents him with a beautiful silver shield to match the sword previously given him and it ends in a bear hug that they will both long remember.

"As Ralph starts on the long journey home he remembers the first parting from Garth and how they learned to help each other. This time they are able to achieve even more without the need to explain what each was doing. Ralph finally understands just how important it is having a friend to support you in reaching your goals.

Tatiana

The King of the Jungle

The Supreme Bear Council

Dr. Hamilton arrives at the hospital and goes directly to SJ's room. He notes that Genevieve and her mother are both there and sees that SJ has gone into another staring fixation. He walks over close to the bed and claps his hands together, as loud as he can, just once. SJ jumps at the loud sound, but does not move for probably another minute. And then she slowly moves as if waking from a drugged sleep.

When she sees Dr. Hamilton she asks, "Is it time for another ordeal?"

Dr. Hamilton looks around for Granma and opens his hands in a gesture of 'well?'

Granma comes over to the bed and kisses SJ above the patch over her right eye. "Would you like that, dear?"

SJ tries to shake off the lethargy that comes with her staring fixation, and finally moves to sit up against the headboard.

"I'm ready." She looks at everyone with her lone pirate's eye waiting for the story to begin.

Granma sits down on the side of the bed next to SJ and Dr. Hamilton and Genevieve sits on the chair, set in the reclining position for someone to sleep on it. Dr. Hamilton looks at Genevieve for a long moment, but she only focuses on her daughter and her health.

"Let me see, now. I may not get this all right as I only heard the one story." SJ interrupts, "Ordeal."

"Oh, yes, ordeal is what you call it."

SJ instructs her in the rules, "The bear has to go through up to ten ordeals to be worthy of a little boy or girl. This is the fourth ordeal."

"Oh. I didn't know that. Well a bear told me this story a long time ago, so I may not get it exactly right."

SJ interrupts again, "Is this the bear in the attic?"

"Yes, dear, it's that bear."

"Well he's a little bear so he must have been successful."

Granma looks to Genevieve and Dr. Hamilton, not understanding.

"There's a whole thing about that. I'll explain later." Genevieve reassures her mother.

"Oh. Okay. Please do." Granma turns back to SJ and begins, "The bear found itself in the deepest and darkest woods of Africa."

"Where's Ralph? Where's the Master of Ordeals? How was this one chosen?" SJ interrupts.

"Let me help you with this part, Mom." Genevieve volunteers.

"Ralph woke the next morning after a full and restful night's sleep, knowing he has completed three of his ordeals," Genevieve begins.

"You know I think there are seven ordeals." Dr. Hamilton inserts.

"Seven?" Everyone asks at once.

"Yes, I went back to Charles, my partner, and he talked to his children's bears and they told him they had seven ordeals." Dr. Hamilton informs them.

SJ shakes her head, "My poor bear."

"Well it's not as bad as all that." Dr. Hamilton responds to her, "But more on that later. Let's get on with the sto… the ordeal." Dr. Hamilton winks at SJ.

"All right, now where were we. Ralph woke up the next morning after a full and restful night's sleep, knowing he has completed three of the seven ordeals." Genevieve looks around the room to make sure there are no further dissenting opinions.

"So, Ralph the bear goes to the Supreme Bear Council with his parents and waits as the Master of Ordeals selects the fourth ordeal from the Great Ordeals Mixer. When he takes the ball from the machine, the Master of Ordeals opens it and reads it out loud."

Genevieve looks to her mother for the name of the ordeal, but she doesn't understand so Genevieve asks, "What's the name of the ordeal, Mom?"

Granma, looks at her daughter with confusion, and suddenly she understands and says, "The King of the Jungle Ordeal."

Genevieve picks up the story, announcing: "'The King of the Jungle Ordeal.' There is a collective gasp that Ralph has selected the third most deadly Ordeal. Only three bears have ever returned from the Jungle.

"Well anyway, Ralph looks to his father and says, 'I cannot do this, only three bears have ever returned from the deep and darkest jungles of Africa. And Ralph's father looks at his son and says, 'You have a little girl waiting for you to prove yourself worthy of her. I believe that you will find a way to survive the deepest and darkest jungles of Africa and come back to us. I have taught you many lessons, but the most important is to believe in yourself and to use your imagination to solve problems. I will wait for your safe return'. And Ralph turns to his mother and says, 'Mother I cannot do this, only three bears have ever survived the deepest and darkest parts of the jungles of Africa'. And Ralph's mother hugs her son and says simply, 'Your father and I believe in you'.

"Ralph goes to the Master of Ordeals and asks how to get to the deepest and darkest parts of the jungles of Africa? And the Master of Ordeals responds, "You have to fly American to Gatwick, take the bus over to Heathrow and then catch the British Air flight into Lagos, Nigeria. From there it is an overnight train to the deepest and darkest parts of Africa. Ralph asks the Master of Ordeals, 'Are you paying for these tickets?' And the Master of Ordeals hands him the tickets he bought on Travelocity."

SJ gets upset, Mommy, you're being too…"

"Literal?" Dr. Hamilton inserts.

"Yeah, something like that." SJ concludes, looking for the story to progress.

"I'm almost ready to turn this puppy over to Granma." Genevieve begins, but SJ stops her, "It's not a puppy, it's a bear sto --, err…

ordeal."

Dr. Hamilton smiles, "Gotcha."

SJ smiles, embarrassed that she was caught, but motions for them to keep going.

"So. Ralph the bear has tickets to get to the deepest and darkest part of Africa. But confusion leads him to ask a question. So he asks the Master of Ordeals, 'What do I have to do in the deepest and darkest parts of Africa to prove I am worthy of my little girl?' And the Master of Ordeals says to Ralph, 'You have demonstrated the virtues of Courage and Humanity. In this ordeal you must demonstrate the virtue of Temperance.

"What's temperance?" SJ asks.

Genevieve starts to respond, but her mother keeps on going."

"Ralph asks the Master of Ordeals, 'Does that mean I have to avoid booze?' The Master of Ordeals tells Ralph, 'You obviously have much to learn. Go to the deepest and darkest reaches of the African jungle and discover the meaning of temperance.' And with that instruction Ralph kisses his mother and hugs his father good-bye and boards American flight fifty to London Gatwick."

SJ motions for her mother to take her place back on the sidelines with Dr. Hamilton. Granma looks at her daughter and SJ and remarks, "Oh, is it back to me?"

SJ says, "Take it away."

Granma thinks about the set up and tries to remember how to make it all fit together, but SJ is impatient, "Granma."

"All right child. Let's see now. The bear…"

SJ pipes up, "Ralph."

"Oh, yes, Ralph gets off the overnight train from Lagos in the deepest and darkest part of the African jungle, trying to figure out how he can demonstrate temperance."

Granma looks at Genevieve as if to say, 'Thanks a lot for nothing'.

"So the … Ralph, yes, Ralph the bear wanders into the underbrush and sits down on an ant hill. Now the ants don't think much of this big old brown bear sitting on their hill so they bite him on the … bottom … and Ralph the bear goes running to the nearest lake to wash off the ants that bite him on the…"

SJ pipes up, "Ass."

"What do you know about that?" Granma asks. SJ shakes her head as if to say, I'll never tell.

"So, we find our hero in the middle of a lake in the deepest and darkest part of the African jungle, washing biting ants off his … ass."

SJ giggles when her grandmother uses that word.

"Our hero, Ralph the bear, sits in a lake wondering how to demonstrate temperance to pass this particular ordeal when along comes a Kangaroo."

SJ pipes up, "Granma, there aren't any Kangaroos in Africa."

Granma looks at her granddaughter and says, "Who says? You ever been there?"

SJ shakes her head.

"Then how do you know there aren't Kangaroos in Africa?"

SJ reminds her, "Books, Granma."

"Well you show me the book that says there are no Kangaroos in Africa and we'll change the story to a Wallabies."

SJ pulls her sleeve, "No Wallabies in Africa, Granma."

"How about a Bald Eagle?"

SJ shakes her head, "Don't think so."

"Well what would you suggest my dear?" Granma asks SJ.

"How about a Wildebeest? I don't know what it is, but Mom read about it to me once." SJ responds.

"All right. So our hero, Ralph the bear, sits in an African lake, pulling biting ants off his ass when a Wildebeest wanders by and says to our hero, 'What's a fat old bear doing in the middle of my lake'? Now Ralph did not think of himself as fat or old, but he was willing to forgive the Wildebeest for being so rude and he says to the Wildebeest, 'I'm looking for an opportunity to demonstrate temperance. Do you know how I could do that?' Now of course the Wildebeest had even less of an idea as to what temperance meant than Ralph, but not to be embarrassed by showing his ignorance the Wildebeest replies, 'You could convince the Lions not to hunt us Wildebeests.'

"Now Ralph the bear, our hero, thinks that this sounds like something that would be good to do, pulls the last ants off his ass, climbs out of the lake and goes looking for the King of the Lions. He traverses dangerous terrain, hearing scary roars, and birds calling, and the sounds of large cats snarling, and then he comes to the den of the King of the Lions. So he knocks on the door and Misses Lion invites him in."

"Isn't that a lioness?" Dr. Hamilton asks.

SJ frowns at him so he shrugs.

Granma continues, "Yes, Misses Lion is also called a lioness. So anyway, here's our hero, in the lion's den, at the invitation of Misses Lion and he sees the cubs playing so he joins in their play, especially since he is a very playful fellow. So Misses Lion watches as he plays with the cubs and low and behold the Lion King comes home and roars, 'What's this wimp doing in my house?' Now our hero spends the better part of ten minutes looking for the wimp before he realizes the Lion King is talking about him. Now the bear remembers he is on a mission and he asks the Lion King why he hunts the Wildebeest. The Lion King says to our hero, Ralph, that Lions hunt the animals that would strip the land of its vegetation if they did not control the population of such animals. And if they stripped the land then all animals would suffer and die of starvation. It is the natural order that Lions must hunt those animals that would strip the land of vegetation.

"Now the bear thinks this sounds perfectly logical, but asks if for some reason there were too many Lions, killing too many Wildebeests, would it not make sense for some animal to come and kill them to put harmony back into nature? The Lion listens to his question and tells him that men do that, only they do it too well and there are no longer enough Lions to regulate the other herds. Hearing this our hero, Ralph the bear says to the Lion King, 'Oh mighty King, does it not make sense that if there are not enough Lions to regulate all of the herds that the Lions should choose fewer herds to regulate and that maybe they should leave the Wildebeests for man to regulate?

"The Lion King listens to this argument and agrees with Ralph, the bear, who is our hero, and says, 'make it so, Mister Sulu. Full warp speed to the Klingon galaxy.'"

Genevieve observes, "I think you're mixing your metaphors."

Granma thinks about it for a moment, "Oh. Whatever. Anyway, Ralph the bear, who is our hero, goes back to the lake and tells the Wildebeest that the King of the Lions has agreed not to hunt Wildebeests. Now the Wildebeest is very happy that he will no longer need fear the Lions and the Wildebeest gives Ralph the bear, our hero, a letter to take to the Master of Ordeals saying that Ralph the bear, has negotiated a peace treaty between the Lions and the Wildebeests and in so doing has introduced a measure of Temperance unknown in the deepest and darkest parts of the African Jungle.

"I think you need to finish this now, Genevieve since you know how it ends." Granma looks at her daughter with relief."

"Okay." Genevieve takes the handoff and looks at her daughter. "Now Ralph the bear, our hero, just makes the day train from the deepest and darkest African jungle back to Lagos, Nigeria, where he waits three days for a flight to Heathrow. Once he gets to Heathrow Transportation Security tells him that he has to put the letter from the Wildebeest into check luggage rather than carry it on because one never knows if it might not really be a letter bomb. The problem is that Ralph the bear, our hero, did not have any check baggage, so he has to leave the secure area, go into the outside world, buy an overnight bag, put the letter in it and then check it back in. However, he then must retrieve his bag and hand carry it on the bus to Gatwick for final passage home, although he will have to check in his check bag with the letter one more time at Gatwick."

"Granma, you're as bad as Mommy." SJ impatiently waits for the end.

"So when Ralph the bear, our hero, finally arrives home, he finds that his check bag had been sent to Shanghai by mistake and would be delivered to his home in a week or so. At this point the Master of Ordeals tells Ralph the bear, our hero, that he will have to wait for the letter to arrive to be given credit for successfully completing his fourth ordeal, but from what he tells the Master of Ordeals, it appears that he has demonstrated Temperance through forgiveness of the Wildebeest for calling him fat and old, humility and modesty for not claiming that he negotiated the treaty all by himself, prudence for winning the trust of Misses Lion by playing with the cubs while the King was away, and self - regulation by proposing a scheme that works to the benefit of both the Lions and the Wildebeests. In addition he demonstrated fairness in the terms of the treaty as no one is disadvantaged, and hope in that both the Lions and Wildebeests could hope for better futures under the terms and conditions of the treaty."

SJ looks up at her Granma, "What's the moral of this ordeal?"

Granma looks stumped. Dr. Hamilton suggests, "That you should not wait for someone to bite you in your ass, before you get up off it and do something for others."

SJ smiles, "I like it, but Mommy wouldn't let me say that."

"Clearly not at school." Genevieve agrees.

"So Ralph has completed four ordeals." SJ counts down the ordeals until her bear arrives.

"And they are the four most dangerous," Genevieve reminds her.

"So do I get number five tomorrow? It's your turn Doctor Hamilton." SJ asks.

Dr. Hamilton nods, "I think I can find Doctor Coolidge before that."

SJ smiles, but it fades quickly as she once again becomes tired. Dr. Hamilton notices and asks, "Looks like someone needs some sleep." He yawns to make SJ think he talks about himself. "Night all. Thank you for the sto… the ordeal Misses Wilcox. It was great." Dr. Hamilton waves to SJ as he leaves.

THE ILLUSTRATED BEARMAS READER

The Medusa in the Clouds

The Medusa in the Clouds

Later, Genevieve finds the nurses and Dr. Hamilton waiting for her in SJ's room. She looks nervously around, "You're waiting for me?"

The charge nurse responds as the others nod, "Yup. You're late. SJ here's been waiting patiently for you and the doctor has been doing his best to keep us all entertained without spoiling the story you're going to tell …"

SJ cuts her off, "The ordeal..."

"Right … the ordeal you're going to tell us about. The doctor said you've been working on this all week and even sent to the Library of Congress for a copyright or some such thing. Is that true?" The other nurses all listen for the answer.

Genevieve, shakes her head. "No I haven't filed for a copyright. I'll have to talk to that doctor, starting rumors and all." The nurses react to the news, with one defending the doctor and the other replying that he's always doing things like that just to confuse everyone.

Genevieve drops her things, kisses SJ on the forehead, "You ready, Kiddo?"

"I'm past ready. Ralph can't come until he gets through what… three more ordeals? And if he fails any one he has to go be a redeeming bear and I have to wait more than two whole years?"

"Ralph's a courageous bear…" Genevieve starts.

"Momma." The message in SJ's voice is clear: Time to sit down and tell the ordeal. She complies, situating herself next to an anxious SJ.

Dr. Hamilton smiles at Genevieve. She asks him quietly, "Copyright?" He shrugs innocently. She laughs, shakes her head and then begins to puzzle for a moment as if trying to remember how this goes. A look of remembrance crosses and she starts in.

"So when he woke from a good night's sleep he returns to the Supreme Bear Council with his parents and watches the Master of Ordeals select another ball from the Great Ordeals Mixer.

When the Master of Ordeals opens the ball and reads the Ordeal to Ralph --"

"I hope this isn't too hard." SJ squeezes her mother's hand.

"The Master of Ordeals reads the slip of paper that says only, 'Bring back the jewel of the sun god, Ra.' And all of the bears look to each other with very wide and fearful eyes for they had thought that everyone had forgotten about the sun god, Ra. But there is no rhyme or reason to how the Great Ordeals Mixer selects ordeals or the nature or difficulty of them."

SJ gazes off into the distance, as if trying to picture a large jewel in her mind's eye or at least that is what Genevieve thinks she is doing.

Genevieve continues, "Ralph looks to his father and says, 'Who is the sun god, Ra? I don't know anything about him.'

"And Ralph's father looks at his son and says, 'Beats me, but I believe that you will find a way to recover the jewel of the sun god, Ra and come back to us. Use your imagination to solve this problem.'

"Ralph turns to his mother and says, 'Mother, what do I do?' Ralph's mother hugs her son and says simply, 'Do as your father suggests.'"

SJ looks to her mother and says, "So how did he find the sun god, Ra?"

Genevieve smiles at SJ, "I'm just coming to that. So the Master of Ordeals tells Ralph, "You do not go to the sun god, Ra to find her jewel. It was stolen by the thirteen headed Medusa a thousand years ago. You must find the Medusa and retrieve the jewel."

"But how do I find this Medusa?" Ralph asks.

"'Your transportation awaits you outside.' The cryptic response from the Master of Ordeals confuses Ralph, but also makes him curious.

"Ralph does not know what to expect. A thirteen headed Medusa, a jewel stolen from a sun god he never heard of before. Transportation that awaits him. This poor bear has already been through so much to prove himself worthy of his little boy or girl. But he will not give up now. He must persevere.

"Ralph leaves the Hall of the Supreme Bear Council to find four long necked geese harnessed to a jewel-encrusted chair. He walks up to the nearest of the geese and asks, 'Mister Goose, I need to find the Medusa in the clouds. Can you take me there?'

"The nearest goose looks across to the other lead goose and remarks, 'Hey lefty, this guy wants us to take him to see the Medusa. You paid up your life insurance?'"

"The far goose rolls his eyes and shakes his head as if bears never get it right, 'Of course my insurance is paid up. I wouldn't leave home without it. But the Medusa is another thing all together, now. You remember the last time we took a bear up there? We hardly got away. And that poor bear. I can still see him with his long bladed knife trying to slay the Medusa, but not knowing which head to face. And then the tail came out of nowhere and sent him flying into the great beyond.'

"The near goose turns to Ralph with a look almost daring him to continue on this self-destructive voyage, but either Ralph does not believe the far goose or does not care. A little girl awaits and Ralph must prove himself worthy of her. Nothing, including a many headed Medusa and a blinding fast tail, can dissuade Ralph from his fate and his little girl.

"So Ralph climbs into the jewel-encrusted chair and looking straight ahead, says, trying to conceal the fear in his voice as best he can, 'Take me to the Medusa in the Clouds.'

"The geese, being magical geese, are obliged to do the bidding of whoever sits in that jewel-encrusted chair, and so, as one, they lift off and carry Ralph skywards into the white fluffy clouds, leaving his mother and father watching him disappear from sight."

SJ has trouble picturing the Medusa. "How many heads does this Medusa thingy have?"

Genevieve stops to think about this for a moment, but Doctor Hamilton speaks up first, "She had thirteen heads on long flexible necks. So the heads actually turn and look at the other heads, move in front, to the side or even behind another head."

"That must be weird." SJ sounds like she does not completely buy Doctor Hamilton's explanation.

Genevieve doesn't know how much she should embellish this point so she appeals to SJ's logic. "Well … anyone who lives in the clouds must be a little different from you and me."

"Does the Medusa have wings or something to keep herself from falling?" SJ still does not sound like she has the image clear.

"People thought that thunder was the gods having arguments and that they lived up in the clouds. So I guess the Medusa was another of those supernatural beings that live up there amongst the gods." Genevieve explains. "So, Ralph keeps his head high as the four geese carry him to the cave of the Medusa. But as they make their way to the cave, Ralph looks down at the jewel-encrusted chair in which he rides. He notices that in front of him the jewels form a cross and he reaches down and finds that the cross is actually the handle of a magnificent sword. He withdraws the sword from its resting place and he discovers that in the very end of this handle is the largest dark red ruby he has ever seen."

"How big is that ruby?" SJ suspiciously asks her mother.

"As big as a … tennis ball." Genevieve hesitates before deciding on something huge but also believable.

"You sure it was that big? Ralph must have big hands to hold that."

"Ralph holds the handle and the ruby is below his hand and the blade above it. But let's not get ourselves sidetracked here. Ralph wants to find this Medusa and he now thinks that the geese have given him a magical sword with which to fight it."

"Is it magical?" SJ remains skeptical.

"You'll just have to wait and see, now won't you." Genevieve tries to keep the ordeal moving much to the chagrin of her daughter.

"I don't like to wait."

"None of us do, but Ralph is a patient bear and he would want you to be as well. So back to the ordeal. Ralph decides that if there is a sword, there may be other things hidden in the chair that can help him as well. He finds a gold shield beneath his feet and in the middle of the shield is a large smoky-grey, but transparent stone. As Ralph looks down he sees the ground a long way beneath him now, and his fear lessens. But just the same he does not remove the shield just yet. He wants something to rest his feet on until they reach the cave of the Medusa."

"Is he really afraid of falling?" SJ tries to follow the story.

"He's way up in the clouds by now, so yes, he is a little afraid, but more than that he doesn't want the Medusa to know all the things that he will use to fight her."

"I guess that makes sense." SJ relaxes and waits for her mother to continue.

"Anyway, Ralph continues to look around the jewel-encrusted chair and turns part-way around. He sees a carved helmet with a large red plume coming out of the top behind him and he reaches round to touch it only to find it is really metal and a real helmet. He stands up and puts his knee into the chair seat as he works the jewel-encrusted helmet loose and finally free. Ralph curiously notes that it is just his size, so still with his back to the direction the chair moves, he places the helmet on his head and raises the sword, whose gleaming blade sparkles in the sunlight.

"Ralph turns around to find the geese have arrived at the lair of the Medusa and now fly into the mouth of the cave. It is very dark and scary in here. Sounds like moans and people suffering come to Ralph, but it does not bother him, or maybe he just doesn't know what the sounds really mean. Anyway, Ralph reaches down, now that they are in the cave that serves as the lair of the Medusa in the clouds, and removes the jewel-encrusted shield from the floor of the chair. He holds it up and looks through the smoky grey stone."

"Why is he doing that?"

"Ralph has heard the stories of the Medusa from his father." Genevieve wants SJ to think of this like the stories she reads to her at night and hopes that she will make the connection as he does not want this to be too scary, but it has to be an ordeal none the less.

"Did Ralph's father ever meet the Medusa?"

"No, but there are always legends. And this was the legend that his father had heard."

SJ nods as she thinks about this and her mother gives her a moment before continuing.

"So why does Ralph look through the smoky colored stone?"

Genevieve knows SJ is ready for this part of the story now, "The legend is that the Medusa can turn a bear to stone with just a look from a particular one of her many heads. This head always has her eyes closed, and only opens them when she feels threatened. If she were to open her eyes and look around, she would most likely turn one of the other heads to stone."

"How can she turn things to stone just by looking at something?"

"Well, SJ, no one really knows, because anyone who was there was turned to stone and was not able to tell anyone what he saw."

"Then how do we know the Medusa turned all those people to stone?"

"Maybe it was the geese from the jewel-encrusted chair."

"Maybe the Medusa has a lot of arms and likes to make statues." SJ suggests.

"Possible, but someone or something came back to tell the legend, and said that the Medusa just looked at a bear and was able to turn it to stone or some other inanimate object. So I guess until someone comes back with proof that isn't true we will just have to believe him."

Dr. Hamilton sees that SJ thinks about this. "Okay," arrives a moment later.

"So Ralph enters the lair of the Medusa in the Clouds. The geese land and wait for Ralph to exit from the jewel-encrusted chair, but he hesitates. 'This is as far as we may take you,' the near goose explains to Ralph.

"'Why is that?' Ralph asks the goose.

"'We are not permitted to enter the chamber of the Medusa, which lies just ahead. Only the bravest of the brave may enter there and we are mere transporters of those who would challenge the great and glorious Medusa.' This sounds reasonable so Ralph steps out of the chair, but hesitates before walking off to the chamber.

"'You will wait for me here?' Ralph asks the near goose, who looks across to his mate.

"'He wants us to wait for him Lefty. What should we do?'

"The other goose again rolls his eyes as if all bears are either naïve or stupid, but he is not a mean spirited goose, in fact he really is just a silly old goose, so he agrees by saying, 'We can wait one hour at which time our meter runs out and since I didn't bring any change I guess we will have to leave. Besides we must return for the next Medusan challenger anyway.'

"Ralph looks at the geese and has to ask, 'You don't bring many back, do you?'

"The far goose thinks for a moment before responding, 'Nope, can't remember the last one.'

"Ralph nods to himself, 'If I have not returned in one hour then you will be justified to leave me here, a statue like all the others before me.' And with that he holds the shield up, looks through the smoky gray stone in the middle and walks into the lair of the Medusa in the Clouds."

"Isn't he afraid? I am." SJ shivers and Genevieve gives her a hug to comfort her before continuing on.

"So Ralph noiselessly creeps forward keeping the shield in front of himself, hoping that the smoky gray jewel will keep him from being turned into a stone should the Medusa open its eyes and see him."

"Why does he think the jewel will do that?"

"He doesn't know if it will, but he has to believe that the shield was there for a reason and maybe he was the first to discover it, for if others had, he did not think that it would still be on the chair. It would be somewhere in the lair of the Medusa."

SJ looks at Dr. Hamilton who nods in agreement, so she turns back to her mother expectantly.

"As Ralph enters the room the first sight of the thirteen heads of the Medusa is more horrible than Ralph ever considered. The Medusa sleeps with each head lying on a pillow of silver threads, with each uglier than the last and the smell of the unwashed monster overwhelms Ralph. He stumbles and chokes at the same time, making enough noise that half of the heads rise up and open their eyes to see who enters the lair.

"Ralph regains his footing and raises the shield just as the many heads comprehend that they have company. The many Medusa heads look at Ralph expecting something, but nothing happens. They gaze upon each other clearly confused and yet curious. Ralph steps one step closer and all of the open eyes of the Medusa return to him. And as they do, a strong rush of flame passes over his head. Ralph realizes that without his magical helmet his fur would have singed from the flames. He touches the helmet still on his head and finds that the fine red feather that had gloriously adorned it has vanished. All that remains is a thin spine of what had been the feather.

"Ralph scrunches down below the shield and watches the Medusa through the gray jewel in his shield. The Medusa has become more curious than before and several of the heads extend on their long necks toward Ralph, as if to get a better look at this pesky presence.

"The head that approaches closest to Ralph bellows in a very loud voice, 'And who sent you to disturb our peaceful repose? No one has dared enter our lair in over a century.'

SJ's eye brows furrow. "How long is a century?"

"A hundred years." Dr. Hamilton responds, but Genevieve gives him a look and he sits back as if he understands her meaning.

"That's a long time." SJ remarks.

"Before you were born." Genevieve responds. She tries to restart the story but SJ stops her with a raised hand.

"You said the chair geese were returning for the next challenger, but no one has been there in over a century."

Dr. Hamilton raises an eyebrow. "Hmm, you're quite correct. It must be that the chair geese don't experience time the way we do. They are only dispatched when this particular ordeal comes up and apparently that doesn't happen very often."

"But there are lots of bears going through their ordeals aren't there?"

"Yes, but this must be a special ordeal that most bears do not go through."

"Is that good or bad for Ralph?"

Dr. Hamilton shrugs when Genevieve glances at him for support. "Neither. There are thousands of different ordeals that bears can go through. If everyone went through the same ones all of the time, they would no longer be ordeals now would they?"

"I don't know." SJ seems confused.

Genevieve goes back to the ordeal. "But Ralph is not afraid ... well ... maybe a little, but he answers the Medusa right back, "I, Ralph the Bear, have come to reclaim the lost jewel of the sun god Ra, of which you are in possession."

"One Medusa head moves closer to Ralph while half of the heads remain with their eyes closed. The same head then leans very near Ralph and comes up right in front of the gray jewel in the gold shield that Ralph holds before him ... well actually he shakes nearly uncontrollably behind it, but he does his best to keep the Medusa in the clouds from noticing this. Ralph does not want to convey anything but confidence to the monster.

"Is the monster going to eat Ralph?" SJ wants to know.

"The Medusa usually just turns bears into something. Each head, according to the legend, has the ability to turn each challenger into something different. But maybe ... just maybe, one of those heads is a vampire head and would want to suck blood from his neck. Maybe another head wants to have a bear meat sandwich. With so many different heads, half of whom are still asleep, each with a mind of its own, it's really hard to know what the Medusa would or would not do. Anyway, the Medusa head looks at Ralph with just one eye through the gray jewel in the center of the gold shield. That one eye appears magnified through the stone and Ralph nearly drops the shield when that single huge eye seems to bore right through him.

SJ puts her hands to her mouth, fearful for Ralph.

"Getting a grip on things, Ralph straightens back up, bangs the shield into the Medusa head, which causes it to recoil, and momentarily having the advantage of confusion, he takes another step forward. This causes two more Medusa heads to open their eyes. And as they gaze upon Ralph behind his shield, a mighty gale wind passes through the lair. Ralph drops his jewel-encrusted sword to hold onto the shield with both hands and brace himself against the fierce wind.

"Does the sword blow away?" SJ asks.

"No, with all of the jewels on the handle the sword is very heavy, and that keeps it from blowing away. But … the clattering sound draws the curiosity of the Medusa. Three heads lean forward as the wind trails off. Ralph instantly grabs the sword and pulls it in behind the shield so that the three heads cannot see what he has. One head attempts to peer over the shield, but Ralph lifts it and tilts it back to obstruct the view.

"The Medusa head that tries to see over the shield asks in a very high squeaky voice, 'What do you have back there, Mister Bear?'

"Ralph tries to steady his voice, but he now remembers the story of the quick tail that caught so many bears by surprise and he cautiously looks through the jewel in the shield for any signs that the tail has been sent to dispatch him. Relaxing for a moment, he remembers the question and responds, 'I have only my wits about me.'

"What are wits?" SJ responds immediately.

"Wits are your ability to think quickly. If you can out wit someone, that means that you can think of something to defeat the other person quicker than they can think of something to defeat you."

"I don't understand."

Genevieve continues the answer. "Bre'r Rabbit out witted Bre'r Fox, remember? He told the fox not to throw him into the briar patch as it would be a fate worse than death, knowing all the time that the briar patch was his home. And once he had the fox convinced that it was the worst thing he could do to Bre'r Rabbit, Bre'r Fox threw him into that briar patch and Bre'r Rabbit was as happy as a lark because he escaped the fox."

"So you out wit someone by lying to him?"

Dr. Hamilton answers this one. "By misleading. It's always better not to lie unless that's the only way to outwit someone. Anyway, Ralph tries to outwit the Medusa and her thirteen heads and concealing his magical sword was one of the ways he did that."

Genevieve continues. "So Ralph takes another step forward and asks the Medusa, 'What have you done with the jewel of Ra, the sun god?'

"The Medusa answers, 'It is well hidden, but in plain sight.' The Medusa pulls back the many heads and suddenly the other heads with their eyes still closed rise up and the one furthest back stretches its neck as high as possible and two immense golden eyes slowly open and focus on Ralph. The bear looks through the gray jewel and feels the temperature of the cave drop like a rock. The shield becomes encased in ice and everything seems to stop moving. Ralph watches until the eyes close and at that moment he lifts the shield and rushes forward with the jewel-encrusted sword held high.

"Ralph finds himself directly in front of the startled Medusa who says, 'No one has ever survived the gaze of stone.' The Medusa seems quite perplexed especially staring at the spectacular sword pointed at the throat of the many heads. But then something quite remarkable happens."

"What?" SJ can hardly contain her desire to know the outcome.

"The Medusa looks at the jewel-encrusted sword and remarks, 'You hold in your hand the sword of Ra. The jewel you seek is the ruby on the handle.'

"A surprised Ralph turns the sword up-side-down to have a better look at the jewel at the base of the sword handle. A bright light fills the dark cavern and focuses itself through the bright red ruby turning into pure red light as it comes out the other side of the jewel. The red light bathes the Medusa and before his eyes, she slowly transforms into a beautiful young female bear with light brown fur and a red bow around her neck.

SJ looks in awe at her mother, clearly imagining this scene.

"The female bear looks down at herself and then at Ralph. 'I am Sadie. The sun god Ra changed me into the Medusa more than a thousand years ago. All this time, all I wanted to do is to go home and be with my family.'

"Ralph looks sadly at Sadie. 'But bears do not live to be a thousand years old. Your family must be no more.' And Sadie looks sadder than Ralph ever saw any bear before. But then he has an idea, 'Sadie, I am going through my ordeals to become worthy of a little girl or boy who needs to be comforted. You have endured a thousand year ordeal. Come back with me to the Supreme Bear Council and maybe they will help you find a little boy or girl that you can be worthy of. Then you will have a family.'"

SJ brightens at the thought, "Yes, Sadie needs a family, too."

"So Ralph takes Sadie by the hand and leads her back to the jewel-encrusted chair borne aloft by four geese. As they approach, the geese look at Ralph and Sadie. The goose nearest turns to the other and says, 'Lefty. I hope you waxed your wings because we got double duty going back.'

"Ralph replaces the shield into the floor and proudly helps Sadie up into the chair. Once she settles in, Ralph replaces the helmet above the chair and makes sure it is firmly in place. But Ralph does not return the jewel encrusted sword, needing it to fulfill his ordeal when they return to the Master of Ordeals and the Supreme Bear Council.

Medusa Transforming

"As Ralph settles himself into the chair next to Sadie with the sword on his lap, he commands the geese, 'Take us back on your last flight, as you shall never again need return to this place. The Medusa is no more.'

"The goose nearest turns to the other, 'How do you like them apples, Lefty? He's put us out of business. Guess we will just have to take that job at the Boston Commons as a Swan Boat.'

"And Lefty looks back at the goose nearest and remarks, 'Had to happen someday.' And the four geese rise into the air returning to Earth for the final time, carrying a very happy Ralph and an apprehensive Sadie.

"Where's the Boston Common?" SJ seems to try to remember something.

"Remember the book, Make Way for Ducklings? I read it to you when you were little." Genevieve reminds her.

SJ considers for only a moment, "The Mother Duck and her ducklings that grew into swans." SJ remembers with a broad smile but it lasts only a moment as SJ returns to the story. "But what happens to Sadie?

"The four geese deliver Ralph and Sadie to the Great Hall of the Supreme Bear Council where the Master of Ordeals waits for them to land. Ralph climbs out of the jewel-encrusted chair first and helps Sadie out. He removes the shield with the great grey stone in the center and watches as the geese rise into the air, fly a circle around the Great Hall and wing rapidly towards Boston and the awaiting Commons Lake.

"Ralph introduces Sadie to the Master of Ordeals and all three enter the Great Hall together. Once inside, Ralph reunites with his mother and his father, who both tearfully hug him once more, grateful that he has returned to them. His mother asks, 'And who is this?'

"Ralph introduces Sadie, but speaks more to the Master of Ordeals than his parents. 'This is Sadie. She is far more worthy of a little boy or girl than I for she has endured a thousand-year ordeal.'

"'And what was that ordeal, Ralph the bear?' asks the Master of Ordeals.

"Ralph presents the jewel-encrusted sword to the Master of Ordeals. 'This was the object of my ordeal. The jewel you seek is the ruby in the handle. It held the power to transform Sadie into the Medusa, which she became for ten centuries. I discovered it in the jewel-encrusted chair and took it back into the lair of the Medusa. There, the sun's rays passed through the jewel once more and transformed her back into the bear she once was. And ten centuries as a thirteen-headed Medusa is an ordeal that should make her worthy without enduring further trials.'

"The Master of Ordeals listens carefully to Ralph's story. 'You speak eloquently, Ralph, and the Supreme Bear Council shall take your recommendation under consideration, but I cannot tell you what their decision shall be. I can only tell you that you have successfully completed your fifth ordeal. Your family is justly proud of your accomplishments. You have once again displayed virtues important to a worthy bear. And your modesty in speaking of the ordeal of Sadie has not gone unnoticed. It is time you rest and prepare for your next ordeal, as it will far exceed the gravity of those you have endured so far. Return when you are ready for your most difficult and most severe test.'

"Ralph wants Sadie to return with him to his home, but the Master of Ordeals leads her away and both Sadie and Ralph shed bear tears at their separation."

SJ looks at her mother, "Ralph really likes her, doesn't he?"

"Yes, he does."

"Will he ever see her again?"

"We'll have to just wait and see what fate they share, won't we?"

"I hope they meet again. Maybe they could share a little girl?"

"I bet you'd like that wouldn't you?"

"Then Ralph wouldn't be lonely for other bears." SJ looks sheepishly at her mother, who gives her an affectionate hug.

SJ looks at Dr. Hamilton. "What was the moral of this story?"

"I like to think it's that you have the power to change your own fate in your hands. When everyone thinks you're doomed to failure, you still have the power to decide what to do and find a way to succeed."

"So I can get well, even if no one thinks I can."

"That's right SJ. You have that power. And when Ralph arrives he will be able to show you how."

The Lotus Eaters

Lorelei in the woods

Dr. Hamilton paces around the room talking on his cell phone to his partner. "I understand, Charles, but this is important too. Can't you get one of the others … Harry, maybe…?" He listens for a moment before continuing, "Well if not Harry, how about Robert? I know he's not doing anything tonight because he told me he was going to go home and just smoke a cigar and drink a bottle of wine … yes, all by himself. Who did you think he'd be sharing those delights with?"

SJ sits up in her bed, waiting for her mother to appear. The charge nurse and the aide who bathes SJ sit on the chair-bed.

Genevieve appears in the door and a smile comes across her face as she sees SJ sitting there watching her with her one eye. "Must be time for an ordeal," she remarks.

"Yes. And Doctor Hamilton's been waiting for you so he can start, so sit down here. Ralph's getting anxious." SJ pats the bed next to her.

Genevieve nods to the nurse and the aide as she sets her things down. She squeezes Dr. Hamilton's arm as she walks past him while he hangs up his cell phone. She kisses SJ on the forehead and she settles in next to her.

"Let me see. Another ordeal for poor Ralph the bear. Let me think a moment. It indeed has been a while since I thought about this." Doctor Hamilton begins.

"So with a good night's sleep he returns to the Supreme Bear Council with his parents and watches the Master of Ordeals select another ball from the Great Ordeals Mixer.

When the Master of Ordeals opens the ball and reads the Ordeal to Ralph --"

"I can't listen to this part. Tell me what it is later." SJ puts her hands over her ears.

"The Master of Ordeals reads the slip of paper that says only, 'Convince the King of the lotus eaters to help others.' And every bear gasps in horror for no bear ever returned from this dreaded ordeal."

SJ removes her hands, "What's a lotus eater?"

"You heard, you little stinker." Genevieve tickles her daughter who breaks out laughing as she tries to push her mother's hands away.

"Well anyway," Dr. Hamilton continues, "Ralph looks to his father and says, 'I cannot do this. No bear ever survived an encounter with the lotus eaters.

"And Ralph's father looks at his son and says, 'I raised you to do what is right and what is important. You have a little girl that waits for you to prove yourself worthy of her. I believe that you will find a way to visit the lotus eaters and come back to us. I have taught you many lessons, but the most important lesson is to believe in yourself and to use your imagination to solve problems.'"

"Ralph turns to his mother and says, 'Mother I cannot do this. No bear ever visited the lotus eaters and returned. And Ralph's mother hugs her son and says simply, 'Your father and I believe in you.'"

SJ looks to her mother and says, "Where do these lotus eaters live?"

Dr. Hamilton continues, "So the Master of Ordeals tells Ralph he must find the deepest and darkest part of the woods for the lotus eaters live somewhere in that dark and mysterious place."

"Ralph leaves the Hall of the Supreme Bear Council puzzled by the challenge of finding the King of the Lotus eaters. First of all, he does not know where the Lotus eaters live, and he has no idea how to identify the King, even if he finds him. This time the Master of Ordeals was less helpful in pointing him in the direction he must take. Ralph thinks about that for a long time as he walks along and suddenly realizes that he does not know where he is. The road is unfamiliar. The forest is denser than he can remember ever seeing. It is so dense that he cannot see light even just a few feet off the road. Now Ralph is an observant bear and this makes him wonder why light does not penetrate the canopy of trees overhead. So Ralph looks up and sees that the trees are much taller than he remembers seeing in the other parts of the forest where he grew up. Ralph looks around him wondering if the tall trees are just in this one location, but he sees that they extend as far as he can see."

SJ makes a face, turns to her mother and asks, "Why are the trees so tall?"

Genevieve smiles and responds, "We will all just have to wait and see, now won't we?" This doesn't satisfy SJ, but the faces stop and she returns her attention to Dr. Hamilton.

"So Ralph stops and listens to the sounds of the forest, realizing that the normal wind rustling through the leaves is missing. In fact, a strange silence surrounds the bear and this causes him to scan the darkness looking for anything that will provide him a clue as to what he needs to do. Ralph stands in the middle of the road and opens up all of his senses to detect anything nearby. It is not a sound that he reacts to. It is not something that he sees, either. What he reacts to is a feeling, a feeling that something watches him. That something prefers to remain hidden, to study him, to come to understand him without revealing anything about itself. Ralph has a choice to make. He can either, watch and wait for the unseen presence to reveal itself, or let it know he knows it is there and try to engage it on his terms. Being a decisive bear, he chooses the later and calls out, "Hello, I'd like to talk with you." Ralph looks deep into the darkness, not knowing if this is where the unseen presence lurks, but all he has to work with at this point is feelings so he goes with them.

"Ralph now waits patiently and his patience is soon rewarded. At first he does not see her as she dresses entirely in black and she moves very slowly. But soon her white face appears almost like a ghostly image suspended in the black forest directly in front of him. Ralph's eyes widen as he watches more and more of her become visible and finally step from the forest onto the road. 'I am Lorelei.' This beautiful woman with long black hair, expressive eyes and a silky voice almost sings her name.

"After a moment to take her in, Ralph recovers and responds, 'I'm looking for the King of the lotus eaters. Would you happen to know where I might find him?'

"Lorelei blinks rapidly a few times and refocuses on Ralph. 'The

King died a long time ago.'

"Ralph considers this for a moment before responding, 'That will make my quest even more difficult.'

"Lorelei turns her head quickly as if she hears something, but then dismisses it and turns back to Ralph. 'And what is your quest brave bear?'

"Ralph looks into the forest to see what caught her attention, but he sees nothing there, even though he looks hard expecting to see at least another floating face. But nothing can be seen. 'My quest is to find the King of the lotus eaters.'

"Lorelei nods understanding part of the dilemma, but not all. "And once you found the King, what did you expect to happen?'

"Ralph suddenly becomes wary of the silky voice and decides to answer cautiously. 'The Supreme Bear Council sent me on this quest to ask the King of the lotus eaters to help us with a matter that I can only discuss with the King.'

"Lorelei's voice becomes even silkier, or so it seems to Ralph. 'I can take you to our Grand Counselor. She will know what to do.' Again, Lorelei becomes distracted by something in the forest that causes her to turn slightly. Ralph's eyes follow hers. This time his gaze is rewarded. A dozen floating faces gradually appear all around him. The others do not emerge as Lorelei has, but rather remain only an apparition, or so it seems to Ralph."

SJ cannot wait longer. "What's a appa-whats-it?"

Dr. Hamilton nods in understanding of her confusion. "An apparition. It's something that appears before you. It generally isn't real, just something that you think is there. It often is your mind playing tricks on you."

"How does my mind play tricks on me?" SJ curiously responds.

"Lots of times when you're in a hurry you may only see part of something, so your mind completes the image. How it does that may or may not be the way the image really looks."

"Like what?"

"Well ... if you were to glance up at clouds in the sky, you may see what looks like a face. What you're really seeing is a shape of clouds with some of the same outlines as a face. But your mind fills in the blanks to make it fit patterns that you expect. If you look at that cloud closer, you realize that the pattern is far from complete and the cloud really doesn't look like a face. And as the winds blow the clouds change shape and begin to look like something else, which may suggest some other pattern that you have stored in your brain."

"But what does that have to do with an app-a-whatcha-ma-call-it?"

"The apparition is something that, like the clouds, appears to be there, but really isn't. In this case Ralph thinks the floating faces are just an apparition, but in fact, they are real and they are there."

"How does Ralph know that?"

"Just listen." Dr. Hamilton continues the story. "Lorelei nods to the faces in the forest and one-by-one they wink out like stars in the early morning sky. And then it is just Lorelei and Ralph standing on the road, facing each other expectantly. Then Ralph remembers and asks, 'Who is your Grand Counselor?'

"Lorelei returns her full attention to the bear. 'She was the wife of our late dead King.'

"Ralph puzzles for a moment, 'But wouldn't that make her the Queen?'

"Lorelei answers simply. 'No, she was not the Queen. Please come with me as soon the sun will set and it is not safe to be here then.'

"Ralph decides that there is much that he does not understand and that he needs to learn more in order to complete this ordeal. 'Why won't it be safe after sunset?'

"Lorelei takes his paw and leads him into the dark forest, answering his question only after they have lost sight of the road and the light that shone upon it. Now it is so dark that Ralph cannot see his guide, He can only follow along behind, led by the firm pressure on his paw. 'Perhaps she will show you what lurks in the night. Perhaps she will spare you. If I were you, I would not be too eager to know the unknowable.'

"Ralph holds on tightly to Lorelei's hand, realizing that if they were to become separated that he might never find his way back to the road. He might also encounter whatever it is that lurks in these woods, making it unsafe after sunset. But Ralph wonders what the sunset has to do with it, as it is as dark as night all the time in this strange forest."

Dr. Hamilton sees SJ shudder at his description of the dark forest and the realization that she is relating to the danger drives him on. "Without warning, Lorelei moves faster, dodging trees and other obstacles. Ralph is not used to running just on his hind legs and finds his little legs pumping furiously to keep up. And still she goes faster. Ralph clings to her hand, afraid that he will lose his one thread to hope and finding the lotus eaters. But now Lorelei moves so fast that Ralph's feet do not always touch down as she pulls him along like a rag doll.

"Ralph clasps her hand with both of his front paws. Now one of his hind feet only touches down once in a while. The bear wishes that she would simply stop, pick him up and carry him with her, but he is so out of breath that he cannot ask the question. He feels his little heart pumping away furiously and he becomes afraid that if she does not slow down soon it just might burst.

"Turning his head, Ralph sees other white faces moving through the forest like ghosts upon unseen black stallions. He thinks he might be hallucinating, but he remembers the dozen or so others that appeared at the road, and he realizes that they are traveling with them to whatever the destination is. To see the Grand Counselor, whoever she is, to come to a resolution of his quest, however that will come out. Maybe they are just along for the entertainment. Maybe they just want to see what she will do to him. *Do these people eat bears?* The thought catches Ralph by surprise. He had never considered that before. And the fact that he does not know if people eat bears worries him. But he feels like he is losing his grip on Lorelei. He pushes harder on the rare occasion that a foot really does touch down in an attempt to ease the strain on his grip, but it does not help. He tries to call to her, but he is so out of breath that nothing comes out, He tries squeezing with all of his strength … to hold on, hoping that they are near the end of this particular journey, so he can rest. So he can regain the strength in his paws that seems to have left him in the dark of this forest, along with all thoughts that he knew what he was doing.

"And then as Lorelei swings to her left to avoid a tree or some other unseen obstacle, Ralph thinks he sees a glimmer of light. But it is not the light of the sun. It looks more like the light of a fire. *It would have to be a big fire to generate that much light.* But Ralph is not sure if it is real or his mind playing tricks on him. He fears it might be another apparition, like the others that proved to be real. He hopes against hope that this one is real as well.

"A turn to the right and there it is again. The apparent fire is bigger … closer now. Ralph becomes more optimistic that it might be real, but still he has to grit his teeth to hold on to Lorelei's hand. He has to concentrate with all his strength, both mental and physical. He closes his eyes, and is surprised that it doesn't seem any different … pitch black … so he opens them again and catches still another glance of the light up ahead. Now Ralph is sure that they are approaching something … the destination, he hopes. And only now, for the first time Ralph realizes that he will be dependent upon these people to lead him out of this place as he has absolutely no idea how he got here or even where here is.

Lorelei and Ralph

"Lorelei begins to slow and Ralph's feet touch the ground much more often, although they still spin like a windmill, hopping and bouncing along. And still she slows more and soon Ralph is merely running along like any other bear pulled along by a fast moving human.

"The fire illuminates a large structure, of which Ralph can, only just barely, make out the outline. There seems to be a large chair on the other side of the fire, as if this were the place where someone watches the fire. *But why would anyone want to sit and watch a large bonfire?* Ralph now trots behind Lorelei and with a turn of his head can see the others are in fact quickly walking in the same direction, that is, directly to the bonfire."

"Who are the others?" SJ wants to know.

"Wait and we will get to that." Dr. Hamilton reassures her. "As they walk into the light aura of the fire, Lorelei releases Ralph's paws and he stumbles and falls facing the flames. Lorelei turns to look at him, but does not offer any assistance. In fact, she backs away and melts into the shadows. Ralph senses that there are many more people about, but that they are also hanging in the shadows, not wanting to reveal themselves or their numbers to this uninvited guest."

"Why don't they want Ralph to see them?" SJ demands.

"Because they can better control the situation when Ralph doesn't know much about what's going to happen." Dr. Hamilton explains, but he looks up at Genevieve, who looks right back at him. The unexpected admiration that he sees in Genevieve's eyes causes him to loose concentration. "Uh … hmmm. Now where was I?"

"Ralph doesn't know much." SJ tries to help him get restarted.

"Ralph?" Dr. Hamilton has to break his gaze with Genevieve to gather his wits and this he does with some difficulty. But when he finally accomplishes it, he has to think for a moment to figure out where he is. "Yes, Ralph. Hmmm … the fire, oh, yes. So Ralph lies on his tummy in front of the fire and no one else can be seen. Is that right?"

"That's what you said." SJ seems confused as to why he seems confused.

"Okay. Anyway, Ralph gets up and brushes the dirt off his fur as he waits to see what will happen next. It is less than a minute before another woman, who looks very much like Lorelei, but her hair seems shorter and her face seems more round, at least to Ralph, stumbles into the firelight, and falls to the ground. Three more women, all dressed in black, all with long black hair, and carrying long rods with a small decorative cap, follow her and stand over her with a menacing posture. The woman on the ground sits up and glances at her guards, pulls herself into a Yoga-like sitting position and apparently begins to meditate.

"Everything is quiet, but there is a sense of anticipation. Ralph can see it on the faces of the guard. He can sense it even in the woman who waits. She meditates, but Ralph senses that this is only something to do while she waits. And it is not long before a trumpet blares a strange tune, and in a moment a red-haired woman, slightly larger than the others, but just as beautiful, enters the light and climbs up into the chair on the other side of the fire.

"The red-haired woman calls in a commanding voice: 'What has Andrea done?'

"One of the guards raises a branch with round green leaves as she talks. 'Andrea refuses to eat of the Lotus plant. She claims that she no longer needs a false reality. In fact she claims that the world is a beautiful place without the prism of the plant showing us the inner sanctity of life.'

"The other guards chant in unison, 'The prism of the plant shows us the inner sanctity of life, it gives us order and purpose and strength to protect our reality from those who would steal it away.' All three guards bang their rods on the ground in unison, three consecutive times.

"The first guard raises the branch once more. 'She is a heretic. She believes that the plant that is the source of our altered consciousness is not divinely created.' A collective gasp fills the air, coming from a crowd of unseen observers who Ralph estimates must number in the hundreds. 'She is a heretic for she believes that it is we who have created a false understanding of our world. She suggests that the larger world reflects a diversity of beliefs, all embraced by the one true God, who leaves us here only to find a way to live together in peace and harmony.'

"The other guards chant in unison, 'The prism of the plant shows us the inner sanctity of life, it gives us order and purpose and strength to protect our reality from those who would steal it away.' All three guards bang their rods on the ground in unison, three consecutive times.

"The first guard raises the branch once more. 'She is a heretic. She believes that men are equal to women and should be given equal responsibility along with their freedom.' A second collective gasp rises from the unseen one hundred or so shadows.

"The other guards chant in unison, 'The prism of the plant shows us the inner sanctity of life, it gives us order and purpose and strength to protect our reality from those who would steal it away.' All three guards bang their rods on the ground in unison, three consecutive times.

"At this Ralph raises his paw, but is ignored by all those whom he can see. 'Excuse me? Might I ask a question?'

"The red-haired woman turns and notices Ralph for the first time. 'And who is this bear? Who brought him to our forest home?'

"Lorelei steps back into the light from the shadows. 'I did Grand Counselor. He is sent by the Supreme Bear Council to ask your help.' Lorelei bows her head and steps back into the shadows.

"The Grand Counselor turns away from Ralph and back to Andrea. 'One thing at a time. The next you know we will have to multi-task, again. That was our downfall, thinking that we could do everything a little at a time and get everything done. That fallacy has been demonstrated. We are now stronger and in control because we learned the power of One Thing at a Time. We have rendered them subservient by forcing them to multitask. They are incapable of doing it all, just as we were. And their inability to succeed has been the secret of our rise to power. And now we dominate them by day ... but enough. Andrea. You are a heretic. You would have us abandon the true life to return to the reality we chose to leave those many centuries ago. The lotus plant gives us our power. It gives us our strength. It gives us insights into the world that the other creatures of this world cannot dream of. Why would you have us abandon that which makes us great?

Why would you have us embrace those who have false gods and false beliefs? Why Andrea?'

"The woman on the ground opens one eye and stares straight ahead. After a moment the other eye opens and she eventually looks up at the red-haired woman. She rises to her feet and stands defiantly before her and the three guards and their long rods. 'History is full of those who disbelieve. Sometimes they are proven wrong, but in all too many cases we find that it was indeed the rest of the world that was wrong. Our society is built upon a dream. This dream is chemically induced and clouds our perceptions of reality. You say that the Lotus makes us free, but I disagree. I have voluntarily chosen not to eat the Lotus any more. I have been able to see the world through my unimpaired senses. I can see that there is much that is not good. I can see that not everyone is beautiful. I can see that things should be different, but not my sisters who are slaves to the plant and the prism it makes us view the world through. I say that we have the opportunity to be free. Really free. Of the tyranny of the plant. Of the tyranny of false dreams. Of the fear that we all live in of the night, even though we live an existence darker than the night, and more fearsome.'

"The red-haired woman rises from her throne. 'My late husband, our King, made us his slaves. We threw off the yoke of male dominance. We have returned the lotus eaters to the matriarchal society that predominated for thousands of years before men found a way to overthrow us. If we give up the Lotus life, men may find a way to regain the upper hand as they once did. Our chemically induced society is the only true life. We cannot go back. We cannot permit heretics in our midst. Andrea, you are my sister, but we cannot permit you to preach a false gospel that may tear our society apart. You must suffer the consequences of your departure from the one true path.'

"The guards chant in unison, 'The prism of the plant shows us the inner sanctity of life, it gives us order and purpose and strength to protect our reality from those who would steal it away.' All three guards bang their rods on the ground in unison, three consecutive times. Then they take Andrea by the arms and lead her to a stairwell. Climbing to the top they come out on a terrace that overlooks the courtyard below and specifically the bonfire, which is directly below. The guards push Andrea, who falls into the fire and is instantaneously consumed by the roaring flames. Andrea's screams rise to a pitch for only a few moments and then die away."

"Why did they do that?" SJ has tears in her eyes as she looks back to her mother.

"Some people are not tolerant of others who are not like them." Genevieve tries to explain, but she can see that SJ is not satisfied. "SJ, you know how when you're sick people stay away from you because they don't want to catch what you have?"

SJ nods.

"Well in this case Andrea had an idea disease that they didn't want others to catch because they were afraid that it would threaten them."

"Was Andrea sick?" SJ tries to understand.

"Well, the red-haired woman thought she was and that was all that mattered."

"But why did they burn her?"

"Do you remember our discussing the witches of Salem?"

SJ brightens, "Oh, yes. The witches made everyone afraid."

"What happened to the witches?"

SJ sounds more somber remembering, "They burned them at a stake."

"The red-haired woman thought that Andrea was a witch of sorts."

"But you said those women in Salem weren't really witches."

"And they weren't, but people were afraid of women who were different and when they were at a loss for explanations for things that happened, they attributed them to the women and the witchcraft they thought they performed."

"So Andrea wasn't a witch?"

"No, dear. She wasn't a witch, just someone who believed something that was not popular with those in control."

Dr. Hamilton nods upon the conclusion of this discussion. "Are we ready to get back to the story?"

SJ turns back to the doctor and waits for him to restart.

"Dr. Hamilton winks at Genevieve, "Okay. So here is Ralph standing next to a bonfire where one of the women has just been burned for not sharing their beliefs. Of course Ralph is a little nervous about being the next into the fire, but he tries not to show it. He raises his paw again. 'Excuse me? Can we move on to the next thing now?'

"The red-haired woman turns her gaze upon the bear and in that same commanding voice responds, 'Now who are you?'

"Ralph does his best imitation of a gracious bow. 'Ralph the bear at your service. I was sent by the Supreme Bear Council to ask your help.'

"The red-haired woman looks in the shadows for Lorelei and stares for a moment until she comes out of the shadows and bows her head before speaking, 'Yes, Grand Counselor'

"The red-haired woman sounds contemptuous, 'You brought a bear to me without knowing what he truly wants?'

"Lorelei keeps her head bowed as she responds, 'A bear is not sly like a fox. Nor is a bear merciless like a tiger. A bear is honest. When he says that he wants our help, I believe that we should accept that as true.'

The harsh gaze of the red-haired woman leaves Lorelei and returns to Ralph. 'So mister bear, you have beguiled at least one of our number. What is the help you seek from the lotus eaters?'

"Ralph hesitates as he thinks about how to make the request, decides there is not one good way to ask and simply does. 'Bears comfort sick children.'

"The harsh gaze of the red-haired woman lessens and she listens with fewer resistances. 'We are aware of that. We sometimes have sick children of our own and your cousins are a great comfort to them.'

"The lump in Ralph's throat eases and he finds he can talk easier. 'But many times the sick children experience severe pain or emotional disorders which are very difficult to calm. There is a shortage of medicines that help these very sick children. And in some instances their parents cannot afford the medicines that are available.'

"A nod of the head indicates that the red-haired woman understands. 'We treat our children with the fruits of the Lotus blossom. This eases the pain and helps even the most distraught child calm down and heal the underlying cause.'

"Ralph knows he has to ask the question which the red-haired woman has alluded to, possibly without realizing it. 'The Supreme Bear Council would like you to donate your Lotus blossoms to the poor and needy sick children who cannot afford the treatments that would otherwise be available to them.'

"The red-haired woman instantly rises and looks over the flames at Ralph. 'You cannot be serious. Our society is dependent upon the fruits of the Lotus blossom to maintain our peaceful nature. We were once fierce tribes who regularly killed members of the neighboring tribes to right some slight or imagined wrong. Since we began to eat the fruits of the Lotus blossom there have been no wars, no crime and no strife amongst us. You would ask us to give this up so that you can ease the pain of young children whom we do not even know?'

"Ralph nods his head."

"A consultation with the shadows brings the red-haired woman's attention back to Ralph. 'How is your proposal any different from what Andrea suggested just before we burned her in the fire?'

"Ralph also consults the shadows, although he is unable to see anything in them, but he has the clear sense that they are all there and waiting for his response. The wrong response and Ralph knows he will be joining Andrea in the fire. 'It is different because I am not saying that your beliefs are wrong. I am not trying to say that I have a better set of beliefs or even a different set of beliefs. What I am asking is that you expand a belief that you already have … that the fruits of the Lotus blossom can help sick children in pain or who are suffering. I am asking that you rise to a higher purpose. That you look beyond yourselves and help ease the pain and suffering of children, who through no fault of their own, find themselves having to deal with something that each of us would have a difficult time handling.'

"The red-haired woman does not even wait a second before her response. 'Out of the question. We cannot give you what you want without destroying that which we have created. There are only so many Lotus blossoms. We have enough for us, but none to spare. No, mister Bear. You must find someone else to help your children in pain. We will not help you.'

"At this, Lorelei raises her head. "But why not, Grand Counselor?

"This catches the red-haired woman by surprise. It is clear for all to see that she is not used to one of her subjects questioning her decision. 'Did I hear you correctly Lorelei? How dare you question my decision? Just who do you think you are?'

"Lorelei stands her ground even though Andrea remains in the blazing bonfire that roars between her and the Grand Counselor. 'We are a democracy. We all have a say in the decisions that we as a people make. I would not arbitrarily question a decision that is made upon due consideration, but there has been no debate. There has been no asking our sisters if they have an opinion on this subject. It is a question that needs to be asked. Are we just narcissistic women who care only about ourselves and our matriarchic society? What we always thought was good about what we created is that we are truly a sisterhood. A sisterhood is caring. We care about each other as women. We care about each other as mothers. We care about each other's children as an extended family. We even care about the men in our lives, if only to keep them subjugated and servile. But underneath it all we are caring individuals. How can we turn our backs on children in pain, children who suffer from disease and trauma? Above and beyond our Lotus ethic, we are caring individuals and I for one think we should give our Lotus blossoms to the children who need them much more than we do.'

"Now the red-haired woman becomes afraid. An idea has penetrated her world that she is not prepared to stop. It sticks like a dagger into the very heart of her power and the grand concepts that enable her power. She does not have a good idea of how to respond since Lorelei was the other woman to receive votes from her sisters to be the Grand Counselor. She has to take her ideas seriously and yet maybe this is the opportunity to get rid of her once and for all. 'Who among you would destroy all that we have built? Who amongst you besides Lorelei?' she asks.

"The apparitions emerge from the shadows, first as white faces and then as black shrouded figures each with long flowing black hair. At first they do not indicate a response to the red-haired woman's question. But then one hand goes up. That woman looks around defiantly as the red-haired woman stonily watches to see what will happen. Then another hand goes up and slowly all of the hands come up, one at a time to indicate agreement.

"The Grand Counselor cannot believe what she sees. It is the voluntary destruction of the lotus eaters, fed by their own humaneness. The red-haired woman had not seen that a conflict of such core values could be resolved in favor of the larger more general society at the expense of their own unique culture. Lorelei silently crosses the courtyard and ascends the throne as the red-haired former Grand Counselor steps aside. 'Sisters. We have spoken. From the bottom of my heart I thank you for the courage to do what is right. We must devise a plan to provide our Lotus blossoms to the neediest of sick children. Mister bear, would you help us with this task? Once it is complete then we will send you back to the Supreme Bear Council with our pledge of aid.'

"Ralph enjoys the next week as the guest of the lotus eaters, helping them to make their plans. It is during this week that Ralph discovers the secret of the sunset. All of the men are nocturnal, which is to say that they sleep during the day and work through the night. They learned this behavior in college and have not adjusted back, since they have become dependent upon the Lotus blossom euphoria, which removes all aggression, but energizes their work. The men are very productive all night long, but that is when they hunt and all of the animals in the dark forest know that they are fair game once the sun sets. Thus, the animals will attack other animals if they believe they are being hunted. For that reason the women all stay home at night while the men conduct the hunt. Ralph enjoys the fruits of the hunt, sampling wild and exotic meats, although he admits that he really prefers nuts and honey over anything the hunters provide.

"And thus Ralph spends his week making new friends and learning about how a different society grew and how, now that the enabler of that society was about to be diverted for a larger purpose, the lotus eaters intend to manage the change that results. Ralph isn't sure their plans will work out quite the way they hope, but he is happy that the sick children soon will have the benefit of the Lotus blossoms to ease their pain and help with their adjustments. And soon he will return home to his mother and father. And soon he will present the plan of the lotus eaters to the Supreme Bear Council and even the Master of Ordeals will recognize that Ralph is close to completing his ordeals and having a little girl of his own.

"But before that, he has to return through the deep dark forest, holding on for dear life and praying that whoever leads him out will not lose their grip, for if that should happen, Ralph will never again be seen or heard from."

"No. He has to return to me. After all he's been through?" SJ almost cries.

Dr. Hamilton smiles at SJ, but continues on. "Anyway, Lorelei picks up Ralph and raises him onto her shoulders. She tells him to hold on tightly for they will be traveling very fast and if he falls off he will most certainly die. Ralph does as he is told, although the only thing he can hold onto is her hair, but he wraps it around his paws and leans down on her head as she moves into the dark and mysterious woods.

"Ralph soon cannot see, but it seems as if Lorelei travels faster and faster. She leans left and right and Ralph hears the wind in his ears and the sounds of the whooshing by trees and other impediments in their path, but Lorelei sees all and knows where she goes, avoiding obstacles that Ralph can only guess at.

"She makes a particularly sharp move to her left and one of Ralph's hands comes loose. He falls off her shoulders, but hangs on with his one good paw, dangling below her face and looking up into the glowing eyes.

"Lorelei discovers him and hoists him back up onto her shoulders without slowing or breaking her stride. Ralph grasps her hair with his other paw and settles into place, hunkering down once more hoping to flow across the path with her.

"Soon the darkness begins to lift and Ralph sees a clearing up ahead with light coming down amongst the tall trees. Lorelei slows and in only a moment she walks into the clearing as if she had been strolling through the trees, although Ralph knows that was far from the case.

"Ralph jumps down and looks back up at Lorelei. 'How can I thank you for all you have done and all you are about to do?'

"It is I who should thank you, Ralph the bear. We have been blind to the world around us, content to live a sheltered and self-absorbed existence. You have helped us see once more that we have an obligation to be citizens of the world and share the secrets we have discovered for the benefit of all mankind."

"And bear-kind." Ralph reminds her.

"She shakes his paw and displays a generous smile, 'And bear-kind.' And in a moment she is gone, once more traversing the dark path between the world of light and the village of dark. Ralph smiles in remembrance of his harrowing journey and begins the long walk home."

A Visit to the Underground

Ralph the Army Bear

That night when Genevieve arrives at the hospital she finds Dr. Hamilton talking with Ralph and SJ.

"But bears can't squeeze into tiny places like that so they have to fish in wide open streams instead." He concludes and when he sees her come in, he stands to greet her. "Merry un-Bearmas, to you."

"Merry un-Bearmas everyone." She comes over, hugs and kisses for SJ and she provides the same for Ralph.

"No hugs and kisses for Doctor Hamilton?"

Genevieve sees that SJ has been planning this. Genevieve willingly provides the hug and kisses to both cheeks, like the French, and he reciprocates.

SJ beams at her small triumph.

"To what do we owe this unanticipated pleasure?" Genevieve asks both the doctor and her scheming daughter.

"Doctor Hamilton thought we should hear about Ralph's last ordeal." SJ tells her.

"I see, and I think it's my turn?" Genevieve is happy that he is here to see her and SJ. *Must be Lynda didn't make enough of an impression.* But then Genevieve wonders if the attraction is her or SJ. *Didn't he say something about his patients being his extended family? But then he always waits for me rather than telling her Ordeals on his own.*

Genevieve stays dressed for this and quickly tries to think what the next ordeal should be. Dr. Hamilton goes to the intercom and presses the button. No one answers, but the nurses and housekeeping staff all start to wander in and either sit on the window sill or lean against the wall. Genevieve sits on one side of the bed and Dr. Hamilton sits on the other side with SJ at the head. SJ beams, but then says to them, "This is the end, Mommy."

"Okay, kiddo. Let me see. Where did Ralph leave off? So Ralph came back with the jewel and the Master of Ordeals gave him the night off. Right?"

SJ nods and shrugs indicating that she's close enough.

"So the next day Ralph is summonsed to the massive Hall where the Supreme Bear Council meets. Here the Master of Ordeals waits patiently for Ralph and his parents to arrive. Now Ralph was so happy to have passed his sixth ordeal that he and his parents celebrated with a honey and berry grog, that was only slightly alcoholic, but enough that Ralph was a little under the weather the next day."

"You mean he had a hangover?" SJ asks.

Genevieve nods to SJ with a smile and continues, "He is a little late and his father is still in bed. The Master of Ordeals is a little annoyed and so he spins the Great Ordeal Mixer twice to make sure he gets an especially hard ordeal. Soon, a larger than usual ball drops out.

The Master of Ordeals smiles when he sees this larger ball and he slowly opens it and reads the ordeal to Ralph."

"Why is the ball larger?" SJ wants to know the significance.

"The Master of Ordeals reads the slip of paper, black paper with white ink, saying only, 'Visit the Underground.' And every bear gasps in horror for no bear ever visited the underground and returned to tell the tale."

SJ looks confused, "Isn't that the subway in London?"

Genevieve shakes her head "Different underground – that's the tube. Well anyway, Ralph looks to his father who has a terrible headache and just arrived. His father holds his head in both paws throughout. Ralph says to his father, 'No bear ever returned from the underground.' And Ralph's father sort of looks at his son and says, 'Your little girl waits for you to prove yourself worthy of her. I believe you are worthy for you are my son and can drink more than I can as you proved last night. I believe that you will visit the underground and come back to us. I have taught you many lessons, but the most important is to know your limit, don't drink and drive, believe in yourself and to use your imagination to solve problems. I know that you will choose to do what is right and what is important. I will wait for your safe return'.

"And Ralph turns to his mother and says, 'Mother, no bear ever returned from the underground.' And Ralph's mother hugs her son and says simply, 'Your father and I believe in you.'

"Fearful of the Master of Ordeals, for Ralph knows that he angered him and that caused him to draw an impossible ordeal. He asks the Master for directions to the underground. The Master of Ordeals replies 'There are many ways to the underground. Most involve making bad decisions, but others involve making noble choices and living or dying, as the case may be, with the results. You must decide how you will arrive in this place.'

"It becomes abundantly clear to Ralph why no bear ever returned. Then he looks at the Master of Ordeals and asks, 'How will I know when I have successfully overcome this Ordeal?'

"The Master of Ordeals replies, 'If you demonstrate the ability to transcend this life you will be deemed successful.'

"Ralph's father listens and is so fearful for his son that he tells the Master of Ordeals, 'Transcendence is impossible.'

SJ shakes her head. "What's Trans-what's-it?"

"Transcendence is going beyond the things that hold you back." Genevieve responds.

Dr. Hamilton intervenes, "People talk about transcending love. That's where you're able to do things for someone you love that you'd never be able to do otherwise. Like your mama is doing everything she can so you can get better. She wouldn't do that for just anybody. But because she loves you, she's making sacrifices she wouldn't for anyone else."

SJ frowns and looks back at her mother. "I love you too, Mama."

Genevieve hugs her daughter with a tear in each eye.

"Well now. Back to the Ordeal. The Master of Ordeals shows anger that a father would question his selection. He replies, 'I will say no more.'"

"Sounds like you're in deep doo doo, Ralph." SJ shakes her head.

"So Ralph, who is even more affectionate, thinking to himself that he will probably never return from the underground, goes to his hungover father and gives him tearful hugs and kisses, and then to his mother who refuses to kiss him goodbye. Ralph says to his mother, 'Why will you not kiss and hug me goodbye?' And she says to her only son, 'I will not say good bye, only so long, that you will come back to me.'

"Ralph cannot believe that his mother will not say goodbye to him, and heartbroken, he leaves the Great Hall. Ralph stops people on the street and asks do you know the way to the underground? Most people simply shake their head as they walk by. One older white haired woman stops and has to think a moment. 'Yes, dear. My husband and I visited London last year. We went everywhere by the underground. They have a sign that says Mind the Gap. I think it was a red circle with a line through it.'

Ralph walks down street after street looking for the red circle sign with a line through it. He stops and asks people if they know where they're supposed to mind the gap? But he people again shake their heads and keep walking.

"It seems to Ralph that he will never find a way to reach the underground, but he sees a man wearing a uniform coming his way. The uniform is green and he has what look like medals on his chest.

"'Could you help me find the underground? I need to endure one more ordeal and then I'll have a Bearmas and a little girl of my very own.' Ralph asks the man who he sees has stripes on his shoulders.

"'Mister Bear my friends and I endure more ordeals than you can imagine, but we help protect every little boy and girl in our country and often in others as well. We would be proud if you joined us and if you're not lucky and skillful, you might end up in the underground, but that's not what we hope for any of our recruits.'

"This is the first person who has said he would endure ordeals and might get to the underground so Ralph follows the man in the uniform back to his office.

"Ralph was happy that he found a way to the underground and he enlisted on the spot, after only one more honey and berry grog, this time courtesy of the recruiter. He goes through basic training where he loses twenty-five pounds and learns to shoot a gun. His platoon is sent overseas almost immediately to a war zone where his team patrols a rural village. On his first day in the village his team patrols along a flooded fast running river. They hear a scream, a splash and a call for help. He has lost so much weight and is in such good shape that Ralph is the first one to react to the sound. In the rapids a little girl, not more than five years old is carried along bobbing under and back to the surface. Her mother calls to her baby from the bridge, and it is clear that the girl fell from the bridge. Ralph does not hesitate a second, he dives into the water and swims as fast as he can against a fast running current to reach the little girl and brings her to a large boulder in the middle of the stream. By the time he reaches her he is too tired to swim back carrying her, so he calls for his team. They come out on the bridge and build a rope chair for the little girl and throw it to Ralph. But the stream is so strong that they cannot get the rope chair to him. So Ralph has them throw it one more time and he swims with all of his strength to where the rope chair hangs under the bridge. Even though he is very tired, he swims back until he reaches the little girl. He helps her into the rope chair and has his team mates pull her back in. But because she is downstream from the bridge, she would be dragged through the water if they just pull on the rope, so Ralph swims with the rope chair and the little girl in it on his shoulders until they are under the bridge. His team is able to pull the little girl to safety and reunite her with her mother. But Ralph is exhausted and cannot fight against the current any longer. The fast moving waters carry him away. Ralph tries to make it to shore, but he is slammed against large rocks in the stream, one after another and he is dunked under and barely has strength to fight back to the surface, and finally he smashes head on into a large boulder and he passes out … and he drowns."

"He drowns?" SJ cannot believe it. "My poor Ralph."

"Ralph wakes up in the underground where he meets Peter the Great. The Great Black Bear that is Peter the Great says to Ralph, 'Why did you save the little girl at the expense of your own life?' And Ralph replies, 'I came to the underground to prove myself worthy of a little girl who waits for me. But if I did not save that little girl in the river, I would not be a worthy bear. So, you see, I had no choice, even if that meant that I might never have a little girl of my own.

"Peter the Great had never met a bear as humble as Ralph and he decided to write a letter to the Master of the Ordeals saying that Ralph visited the underground and that he is the first bear that ever demonstrated transcendence. His actions are so worthy that for the first time a bear that reached the underground is being returned to the world above. Therefore, he recommended that Ralph be recognized as passing the ordeal, and be deemed worthy.

"The next thing Ralph knows he is back home. His mother and

father hug and kiss him for he has been to the underground and returned to them. He hands the letter from Peter the Great to the Master of the Ordeals who reads it to the Supreme Bear Council. They say Hallelujah, for Ralph has demonstrated not only the transcendent virtues of a true bear, but also his worthiness by sacrificing himself for a little girl. And since he is the only bear ever to have achieved that and return from the underground, he is declared worthy, a Bearmas authorized and his ticket to Dallas to meet SJ, his new little girl is handed him by the Master of the Ordeals."

Exhausted from telling the Ordeal, Genevieve looks around and everyone in the room dries a tear, including Dr. Hamilton. Then the nurses both begin to clap together and then the housekeepers join in and SJ grabs her mother and gives her the biggest hug ever.

Overcome by the reaction to the ordeal, Genevieve notices that one of the nurses has a small tape recorder going, which she now clicks off.

She looks back at Dr. Hamilton, who gives her a hug.

"It should be a bear hug." SJ calls out to them. Dr. Hamilton gives Genevieve that bear hug and she hugs him back, thinking it would be nice to have bear hugs more often, like at least once a day.

The housekeepers and the nurses file out, but each one comes to Genevieve and tells her how much they loved the ordeal and how they thought it was better than Dr. Hamilton's ordeal, but they would appreciate it if she didn't tell him that. Of course Dr. Hamilton over hears each one of them saying that, and he just shrugs to them and winks.

As the last one leaves, Dr. Hamilton sits down next to SJ.

SJ looks puzzled, "He won't be a Redeemed Bear, will he?"

Dr. Hamilton doesn't miss a beat, "He will still be a large bear because he has such a big heart that it would never fit in a smaller bear."

SJ nods in understanding, but then asks, "So he can catch salmon and make baklava even though he was never a Redeeming Bear?"

Genevieve nods, "Of course, SJ. Papa bears teach all their children how to fish for salmon and momma bears teach all their children how to make baklava."

Dr. Hamilton smiles at her, "Good answer."

"But I don't have a poppa bear. Does that mean I'll never learn to fish for salmon?" SJ realizes.

"I'll teach you to fish for salmon, as soon as you're well." Dr. Hamilton offers.

"I'm well now. Will you take me tomorrow?"

"Not tomorrow, but soon."

"In Chile? They have rivers with salmon, don't they?" SJ looks directly at Dr. Hamilton to gage his response.

"Sure, if that's where you want to learn to fish, then Chile it is." Dr. Hamilton winks at SJ. Genevieve looks at both of them with a puzzled expression.

Bearmas

Ralph

The next day Genevieve finds SJ on a gurney in the hallway next to the nurse's station talking with Dr. Hamilton. The nurses busily run in and out of SJ's room and finally one nurse comes out and proclaims, "We're ready."

Dr. Hamilton nods for Genevieve to come help him push SJ into her room.

She kisses SJ on her nearly bald and now eye patchless head. "Hi, Kiddo."

Together Dr. Hamilton and Genevieve push SJ into her room to find balloons and streamers hung from the ceiling and a big sign proclaiming: MERRY BEARMAS. The nurses, aides and housekeepers await them in the room, and they clap their hands as SJ comes in.

Dr. Hamilton slides SJ into her bed, arranges pillows so she can sit up by herself, and then raises his hand for quiet. "Does anyone know the story of Bearmas?"

SJ pipes up, "I do."

Dr. Hamilton asks, "But do you mind if I tell it to everyone?"

SJ nods okay.

"Well Bearmas is the celebration of the birth of a bear. Did you know that when little girls and boys are sick or alone and frightened that somewhere in the world a bear is born who is destined to be theirs and theirs alone?" Dr. Hamilton turns to look at SJ, letting everyone know who the recipient will be and to make sure he has her approval, that he has the story right.

"Now that bear has to prove to its parents and the Supreme Bear Council that it is a worthy bear, worthy of being the one special bear for that little boy or girl. The bear has to undergo a series of ordeals where, if it succeeds, it becomes worthy. But if the bear fails even one of the ordeals, the bear becomes disgraced and must join the salmon hunters, the group of redeeming bears. These bears must fish the most remote rivers of Alaska for a year, feeding all of the northern bear tribes. At the end of that year they must then join the baklava bakers, where they gather nuts and honey and make baklava for all of the northern bear tribes. After a year making baklava they have redeemed themselves and become eligible to challenge the ordeals for their chosen boy or girl. But this is their last chance. If the redeemed bear successfully makes it through the ordeals, they come and live with their chosen boy or girl. But if the bear fails at even one ordeal, it is cast out of the bear tribes and must wander the wilderness of the most far northern reaches of Alaska."

Another visual check with SJ, who nods to him and he keeps going. "And that's why sometimes boys and girls get small bears; they're the ones who are successful with the ordeals the first time through. If a much larger bear arrives, then you know that bear did not make it through the first time, but is a redeemed bear. But redeemed bears have many more stories to tell and are also good salmon fishermen and baklava bakers. And that's why when we celebrate Bearmas, we always eat salmon and baklava in remembrance of the redeeming bears."

Dr. Hamilton and Genevieve both wish SJ, "Merry Bearmas."

SJ asks, "Do I get the bear in the attic?"

Genevieve shakes her head, "No, SJ. That bear belonged to your Aunt Yvette. You never met her because she died when she was about ten years old, long before you were born.

SJ seems curious about this, never having heard this particular story before, but she says nothing more.

"Now, Bearmas is not the bear's birthday, but is the celebration of the bear's birthday and the completion of the ordeals that bring the bear to a little girl or boy. That particular bear was loved by your Aunt Yvette. Another bear was born to love and be loved by just you and do you know who bear that is?"

SJ gets wide-eyed as a nurse brings in a big brown bear, nearly as big as SJ.

"Is this Ralph?" She asks awe struck by how big he is.

"Yes." Dr. Hamilton tells her.

"Can he fish for salmon and make baklava?" SJ asks him, at which cue the nutritionist wheels in a cart with salmon, juice and baklava. The rest of the nurses come in for the celebration and join them in their Bearmas feast. One of the nurses brings in a small radio. They play music and the nurses dance while SJ laughs at their uncoordinated efforts. The nurses drag Genevieve and Dr. Hamilton to their feet to join in the dancing and soon the room is full of dancing nurses, all moving in an awfully uncoordinated fashion to rock and roll music.

A slow song starts on the radio and everyone sits down, although Genevieve and Dr. Hamilton linger behind the nurses.

Soon the salmon and baklava have disappeared, only a little juice remains and the nurse takes her radio back to the nurse's station.

SJ's head keeps bobbing as she leans against Ralph.

Genevieve smiles at Dr. Hamilton. "This has to be the best Bearmas ever. I really have to thank you and everyone. I couldn't have done this."

"Thank the Supreme Bear Council. They chose Ralph and this is just a traditional Bearmas feast." Dr. Hamilton tells her.

Genevieve accepts that with a nod of her head, tucks in SJ who keeps her arm partially around Ralph, and kisses her good-night.

About the Author

dhtreichler toured the global garden spots as a defense contractor executive for fifteen years. His assignments covered intelligence, training and battlefield systems integrating state of the art technology to keep Americans safe. During this time he authored seven novels exploring the role of increasingly sophisticated technology in transforming our lives and how men and women establish relationships in a mediated world.

Keep up with all of dhtreichler's latest work and essays at www.dhtreichler.com.

Also by dhtreichler

The Ghost in the Machine: a novel

Life After

The Tragic Flaw

Succession

The End Game

I Believe in You

Rik's

The Illustrated Bearmas Reader – Ralph's Ordeals

The First Bearmas

Made in the USA
Columbia, SC
07 June 2021